David Brazier's tenth book

Buddhism is a Religion:
You Can Believe It

Buddhism is a Religion

You Can Believe It

David Brazier

Woodsmoke Press

Buddhism is a Religion: You Can Believe It
ISBN 978-0-9931317-0-7

Published by Woodsmoke Press 2014

Cover photograph: Adrian Thompson
Design: Kaspalita Thompson

Woodsmoke Press
Amida Mandala
34 Worcester Road
Malvern
WR14 4AA

kaspa@woodsmokepress.com
www.woodsmokepress.com

To

Mahasiddha Chogyam Trungpa Rinpoche
who gave me a method

Reverend Master Jiyu Kennett Roshi
who gave me a faith

&

Reverend Gisho Saiko Sensei
who gave me a mission

Previous books by David Brazier

A Guide to Psychodrama

Beyond Carl Rogers:
Towards a psychotherapy for the 21st century

Zen Therapy

The Feeling Buddha

The New Buddhism

Who Loves Dies Well

Her Mother's Eyes and Other Poems

Love and its Disappointment:
the meaning of life, therapy and art

Not Everything is Impermanent

Sources

This book is written in an easy to read style, accessible to the general reader. Nonetheless, it contains references to, and some critique of, the classical Buddhist sources *The Nikaya Suttas*, especially the *Satipatthana Sutta*, the *Parinibbana Sutta*, and the *Dhammapada*. It also contains references to the works of the Kamakura Buddhist Reformers Eihei Dogen and Honen Shonin from Japan.

The wind that blows through life, unpredictable to us,
rings the bells of Dharma.

Body is unreliable. Mind is unreliable.
Thought is unpredictable. Emotions are wild horses.
The present moment is already passed. The future
is unknown.
History is rewritten each day. No need to mention social
status, wealth, and so on.
Even family and friends cannot travel with us where we
are going.
The one who acts with self-centred mind
lugs along affliction and unnecessary complication like an
old ox-cart.

The one who is fortunate to find a true refuge is
fortunate indeed.
A deep wellbeing attaches to such a one.
For one who stands in the light, happiness effortlessly
attaches to her or him,
like a fine deep shadow.
Let us wish one another such refuge and rejoice when its
brilliant light
breaks through the heavy cloud and be grateful.

When there is light in our lives let us enjoy the shadow,
but, more importantly, have the courage of the light.
When there is darkness let us have patience and faith
in the sun hidden behind the clouds.
The clouds too have their beauty if we will but see it.
Then, without any special virtue on our part
and often unknowingly,
we shall be the hands and feet of a wisdom
far beyond our own.

Sometimes it is joy, sometimes it is grief, sometimes light,
sometimes night.
The bells go on ringing themselves
and we are profoundly fortunate to hear them.

Contents

Preface

There are now millions of people using or having interest in methods, ideas or cultural elements that are derived from Buddhism. It may be meditation, mindfulness, Buddhist statuary, massage, East Asian forms of exercise or medicine, mantric affirmations, or even tantric sex. Buddhism is making significant contributions to Western culture and modern life. This present book may be of interest to anybody who has an enthusiasm for some aspect of Buddhist culture. However, the book is primarily intended to be a support to those who wish to take this Asian religion seriously on its own terms. These are the people with whom the future of Buddhism in the West really rests. It is they who will determine whether Buddhism continues to be a living, vibrant religion with strong roots that continues to yield ever new fruit for individuals, communities, cultures and history, or whether it gets fragmented into so many interesting artefacts to be sucked into the melting pot of modernity, losing its distinctive identity and essential genius.

I have written this book in the hope of giving courage to those, especially in Europe and America, who have a religious view of Buddhism. We have reached the point where it feels almost heretical to assert the obvious fact that Buddhism *is* a religion. Those who cherish it as such stand in the face of a campaign sustained over more than a century that aims to generate a secular vision of Buddhism. There are good reasons why this campaign has been waged and I appreciate them. Further, I am not opposed to people practising whatever faith they wish, nor each doing so in their own way, and to some the notion of a secular Buddhism has a strong appeal. However, we should recognise that such a notion is a creation of modernity. The attempt to represent it as the original Buddhism is unsound. What we currently see in Europe and America is the importation into Buddhism of many values and issues that have no roots in the original religion. This could sometimes be creative and, contrariwise, sometimes Buddhism does have a new and interesting perspective on the age old questions that have haunted Western civilisation. Nonetheless, this is not the original Buddhism and there is a danger that the values and attitude of modernity will swamp the true spirit of the Dharma.

This book is written in the confidence that the core of Buddhist faith has something of immense value to offer to the contemporary world and to the future of civilisation on earth. It does not have to be dismembered and reconstructed in the image of secular rationalism in order to have relevance. Buddhist faith has sustained millions of people through more than two millennia of history. Most of them did not have doctoral degrees; a goodly proportion were illiterate. Many of those people had a faith that modern people can envy. In our sophistication, have we lost sight of the essential? We are, of course, blind to our own prejudices. We tend to put the "enlightenment" of the nineteenth century ahead of the awakening of Buddha.

It is not my intention to turn the clock back. I am not arguing for this or that historical manifestation of Buddhism to be restored. I am arguing for the eternal spirit of Buddhism to be given space and dignity. This means recognising that, whatever else it may sometimes be – a psychology, an education, a culture, a system of healing, whatever – Buddhism is, has always been, and needs to continue to be understood as a religion. This book, therefore, runs against a currently popular trend. There will, however, *be some few who will understand* and this work is intended to give them strength.

Incidentally to this purpose, the book also explains the process of rebirth according to Buddhist belief, makes some, I hope, relevant comments on the importance of bringing metaphysical considerations back into our general discourse, and makes significant points about a number of popular Buddhist scriptures, this latter including a critique of contemporary ideas about mindfulness. The whole will no doubt form part of a debate on questions of secularism and modernity as well as the true nature of the Dharma, a religion that has brought and continues to bring faith and salvation to millions of people.

1: It Needs Saying

It Should Not Need Saying

It should not need saying. After all, it is obvious. Nonetheless, it does need saying. It needs saying because it has been denied by so many people including many who are eminent and even some whose own roles, behaviour and faith contradict what they are saying. It needs saying clearly, that Buddhism is a religion.

Further, this the right time to say it. The band-wagon of secularisation of Buddhism has gradually gathered momentum to the point where it now threatens the whole basis of what the Buddha bequeathed to us. Buddhism is becoming popular, but it is doing so in a form that is a new creation. This new creation is not the traditional Buddhism of Asia and it is not the Buddhism of Shakyamuni Buddha, the founder, either. This new creation is an artefact of modernity and postmodernity using elements abstracted from Buddhism, tailored to gain popularity by satisfying contemporary prejudice.

Having said that, we must add that there is nothing wrong with adaptation and creativity. Many of the new manifestations and applications of ideas and methods derived from Buddhism are intrinsically valuable and can stand on their own feet. Buddhism is like a copious spring, the water from which can be gathered and poured into many different shaped containers. What is problematic, however, is that the reductionist philosophy by which such artefacts are being generated threatens to poison the spring from which the water is flowing. It is a kind of asset stripping, or, we could say, it is like taking the fruit while killing the root.

The basic reductionist principle that informs this process is itself the opposite of Dharma. It is precisely the kind of blindness that Dharma teaching exists to awaken us from. This is why a warning bell needs to be sounded.

I have played a role in the propagation and popularisation of Buddhist psychology so I have a personal part in this process. As somebody who could be seen to be one of the culprits I have, perhaps, a double onus to keep the record straight. Buddhism developed a sophisticated psychological approach two thousand years before the modern world discipline of psychology was invented. Psychological investigations have gone on throughout Buddhist history and the result is a gold mine of knowledge, experience, theory and practice from which we contemporary people can learn a great deal, but although Buddhism has given rise to this treasure, Buddhism is not fundamentally or exclusively a psychology.

My contention in this book is not that we should return to a past that is now irretrievable. It is that while accepting that Buddhism is changing at a cultural level and finding new forms of expression and organisation, we should acknowledge that it is more than merely an expression of modernity using elements of Asian terminology. The most forceful way of doing this is to acknowledge that it is more than a way of life, more than a philosophy, more important and profound than a mere cultural artefact - that it is a religion.

David McMahan made some powerful observations of the contemporary scene in his book The Making of Buddhist Modernism (Oxford University Press 2008). He wrote, "The popular western picture of Buddhism is... an actual new form of Buddhism that is the result of a process of modernization, westernisation, reinterpretation, image-making, revitalization and reform that has been taking place not only in the West but also in Asian countries for over a century. This new form of Buddhism has been fashioned by modernizing Asian Buddhists and western enthusiasts deeply involved in creating Buddhist responses to the dominant problems and questions of modernity, such as epistemic uncertainty, religious pluralism, the threat of nihilism, conflicts between science and religion, war and environmental destruction."

These observations show how Buddhism becomes relevant to the modern world and continues to generate ever new responses to ever new situations. It also, however, illustrates how there is a danger that in making itself relevant it also has to make itself acceptable, and this often means placating aspects of modernism that are themselves the root of the problems that it is addressing, and may represent radical departures from what Buddhism is fundamentally all about. The question at issue, therefore, becomes that of distinguishing what is essential from what is mere presentation. Are we representing the essence of Buddhism in relevant cultural innovations, or are we losing sight of the essence and purpose of Buddhism in the attempt to make it seem relevant?

It is my contention that Buddhism is widely misunderstood and that the root of this misunderstanding frequently lies in the implicit over-valuation of the reductionist tendency of modernity. Buddhism gets shorn of many of its most lively features, and sometimes the cuts go to the very heart of the Dharma body, threatening the life of this most wonderful of human awakenings.

The Fruit is not the Root

For instance, Buddhism is commonly said to be about relieving or abolishing suffering. This can be taken as a worthy humanitarian goal that could have little to do with religion. A methodology that overcomes suffering by training the mind is a psychotherapy. There is, thus, a case to be made that Buddhism is a psychotherapy, and if one were to take abolishing suffering, or achieving happiness, as the goal of Buddhism, then one could claim that Buddhism is primarily, or even nothing other than, such a therapy. Such a line of rhetoric can then be used to integrate Buddhism within the frame of modern, secular, hedonistic ideas. It has been done and it is a successful marketing strategy. Doing so, however, involves discarding most of what Buddhism actually consists of and missing the point of the Founder's original teaching.

Just as it is possible to present Buddhism as a psychology, we can also look at other things that Buddhism has given rise to. Buddhism has generated great cultures that have played prominent parts in history, together with their many constituent ways of life, roles, forms of organisation, social structures, politics, economics and sciences. There is a lot more here than just psychological therapy. There have been extraordinary flowerings of peace, tolerance, creativity and construction. Modern academic investigation finds in this history fascinating areas for study and research. Some modern people adopt aspects of some of these traditional cultures and find it satisfying to do so. They wear Buddhist style clothes, sit on the floor, and have houses full of Eastern artefacts. They study *thangka* painting, or create Zen gardens. Many people now have Buddha figures as garden or household ornaments. These things look fine and contribute to a more gentle tenor of life. Buddhism has given rise to treasures such as these. Buddhism, however, is not fundamentally a culture. It has bred many cultures of great diversity. Buddhism is not fundamentally a way of life. There are many ways of life that can be considered to be Buddhist. Buddhism is not, basically, a style. There are many Buddhist styles. Buddhism has its views of economics and society, but Buddhism is not fundamentally a mode of social welfare. These things are all expressions of something more fundamental. Buddhism is a religion. Only a religion could generate such a diversity of riches permeating every aspect of life.

The Buddha gave remarkable codes of ethics tailored to different groups of people, to monks and nuns, to lay-people, and to those who would follow an altruistic *bodhisattva* path. These ethical codes and studies have continued throughout Buddhist history with new developments in Tibet, China, Japan and elsewhere. The Founder boasted, on occasion, that when he surveyed the contemporary scene in the India of his day he saw nobody who had developed so fine an approach to morality and ethics. To this day we can learn a great deal from this ethical science. We can learn about the better treatment of human and non-human sentient beings; learn about forms of restraint that will benefit the environment, improve our health and longevity, engender harmony in our societies, resolve conflicts, minimise the incidence of punishment and cruelty, and so on. All this is excellent. Buddhism has given rise to treasures such as these. However, Buddhism is not fundamentally a system of ethics. Buddhism is a religion. Without a religious basis, ethics is mere convention.

The Buddha was sometimes referred to as a doctor of the soul, and perhaps also of the body. It is likely that his early disciples, wandering from place to place, not only taught the fundamentals of his doctrine, but also functioned in many cases as healers and medical practitioners. Probably some of the knowledge that they had, such as how to use certain snake venoms as medicine and the uses of a wide range of herbs, may since have been lost, but Buddhism has continued to be an inspiration to the medical arts and many systems of healing have grown up around it. We now think about Tibetan medicine and Chinese medicine particularly. Many modern people are particularly concerned about health. They employ techniques drawn from Buddhism for stress relief, for an improved diet, for deep relaxation, for the treatment of depression, for massage, and so on. All this is wonderful. Buddhism has given rise to such treasures, but Buddhism is not fundamentally a health cure. Buddhism is a religion. The purpose of Buddhism is not stress relief. Buddha did not teach a method to help busy executives survive better in the rat-race.

It is because Buddhism is a religion that it has been able to generate such richness. From the perspective of secular, humanistic materialism it is possible to see a value in many of the things to which Buddhism has given rise, but it is not really possible to see how they have come about because such an approach does not value the processes that constitute the substance of religion and does not recognise the religious nature of the human being. In fact, it consciously, deliberately and systematically excludes them. Humanistic materialism is a reductionist approach which does not admit the dimensions of life that are the fundamental substance of, and springs to action in Buddhism. It is as if a person enjoyed flowers, but considered gardening a waste of time. Flowers are an incidental of gardening and making gardens. Buddhism has a humanistic aspect, but it is not limited to humanism. There is more to the universe than the selfish interests of a single species. Buddhism values secular society, but it is not limited to it. Buddhism has a view of the material world, but it does not see the material world as the whole, or even the most important part, of all that is.

Modernity sees thc fruits of Buddhism as its substance and then wonders how it can be so diverse. The substance of Buddhism, however, is what gives rise to all these fruits and this substance is not part of the materialistic scheme of things. In fact, it involves and is crucially dependent upon a renunciation of such materialism. It is this renunciation that modernity cannot admit, yet which is at the core of the Buddha's dispensation. Even Buddhists who are not renunciants in the full sense of the word, who are not monks or nuns or mendicants, still have as a basic axiom the principle that material considerations are secondary not primary.

In Buddhism, the spiritual is primary and the physical is a domain in which spirit acts. In modernity, the physical is primary and the spiritual, if it is acknowledged at all, is the epi-phenomenon. For Buddhism to survive and continue to produce such wonderful fruit we must not cut off its root in this way. Although Buddhism is, in some respects, very different from the religions we were used to in the past, at core it is a spiritual matter.

A Vision Beyond Measure

Buddhism has a limitless conception of cosmic life, moving through vast cycles in conformity to spiritual laws, in which beings rise and fall according to their deeds in mysterious patterns discernible only by the most spiritually awakened. To enter the spirit of Buddhism is to open oneself to such a vastness of vision, not to close oneself down to a view restricted to what our tiny science has so far been able to dimly discern. The Buddha taught a Dharma or foundation in the form of an opening to wider vision, not a closing down to narrower ones. He taught panoramic, kaleidoscopic consciousness; a religious, transcendental, metaphysical vision that goes far beyond materialism, beyond ethics, beyond self. While valuing the minutest details of life, it transcends all particular worlds, forms and circumstances. While concerning itself with the ephemeral in a spirit of compassion, it is grounded in the unconditioned, the deathless, nirvana. In Buddhism, not everything is impermanent.

This vast vision conveys to us a sense of life as eternally striving through innumerable lifetimes and immeasurable diversity of circumstance toward unconditional love, unconditional compassion, joy and peace. In the fundament of Buddha's teaching, life is meaningful and directional. Direction does not mean predestination: things can go backwards as well as forwards, but it is meaningful and life has purpose within the greater scheme. Nor is this just an individual purpose. In such a vast scheme one can play a part without having to be extraordinary oneself. Furthermore, we can help one another. Buddhism is thus not a post-modern nihilistic relativism.

It is important to establish these points at the start because Buddhism, while it attends to detail, is guided by a sense of expansiveness. It encompasses beings with form and beings without form, worlds we know about and worlds we do not know about, aspects that we can discern and a sense of limitless dimensions beyond what we discern. Buddhism is not about reducing our sense of the universe to dimensions that we can seek to control. It is about waking up to vastness. This includes realising the extent to which so much is out of our control, but being thereby brought to awe rather than dismay. Realising it, we can feel thc most profound gratitude and we can set about ordering our own life from a realistic, which is to say, modest, perspective.

Many contemporary thinkers have asserted that Buddhism is not a religion in order to fit it into our culture. They want to create an American Buddhism or a European Buddhism, in which the encompassing frame is American culture or European philosophy. However, if you cut Buddhism down to fit into one of these frames you cut off the essence and root. It is as if you want to decorate your house with the foliage of a certain kind of tree, as people do at Christmas. They cut the pine tree and bring it indoors and they cut the holly and hang it over the door. By soon after Christmas, however, it is all dead and useless. Buddhism is bigger than the American house or the European house and it has a root that cannot be cut without killing the plant. Buddhism is not something with which to decorate our existing materialistic culture. Using Buddhist methods to help one be more efficient at work, or cope with the stress of a go-getting lifestyle, is decoration of this kind. Buddhism would say, "Have faith in something more wholesome."

The materialist believes in measurement. Things are not important, perhaps not even considered to exist, unless there is a measurement attached to them. Often, these days, the measurement is a price. Buddhism has entered this materialist world sometimes disguised as a saleable commodity. In a world where money is the measure of all things, this is the disguise you need to gain entry. Another measure is popularity. One wins by getting more votes. Votes and prices, however, have no necessary relationship to quality or depth. Buddhism aims to deepen life, not trivialise it. Measures are abstract, useful for some purposes, but never touch the essence of anything. No measure can tell you how beautiful something is. None can tell you how pure a person's heart or soul may be. The science of measurement is valuable and utilitarian. The soul of religion is something else. It is a different domain of existence. It is the one that makes life worth living.

The Religious Aspect is not a Later Deviation

Buddhism has beliefs, scriptures, rituals, prayers, altars, offerings, bells, candles, metaphysics, clergy, devotees, heavens, hells, miracles, relics, meditation, visions, visitations, celestial beings, liturgy, other worlds, other lives, moral law, salvation, saints, shrines, religious festivals, rites of initiation, rites of passage, pilgrimage... need I go on? Nearly all of these are found in Zen Buddhism, in Theravada Buddhism, in Tibetan Buddhism, in Pureland Buddhism, in the other schools of Chinese and Vietnamese Buddhism, in fact, in all of Buddhism all over Asia. Buddhists probably burn more candles and incense than the Catholic Church. These are not degenerations, or cultural accretions. The founder himself gave us robes, taught ritual and contrition, revealed other lives and worlds, and spoke with the gods. Secularised and rationalised variants of Buddhism exist, but it is these that are the partial forms and cultural products of later derivation.

Sometimes it is said that Buddhism is scientific. This assertion would put Buddhism somehow within the frame of science, but Buddhism has much that would not fit into that frame. However, although we cannot really say that Buddhism is scientific, science is Buddhistic. Science is Buddhistic in that science is a way of knowing some things. Buddhism can accommodate everything that science perceives, but science can only perceive a fraction of what Buddhism encompasses: the fraction that appears within the frame that the rules of science restrict one to. Science is wonderful and useful, and even exciting, as far as it goes.

We should not muddle up science and scientism. Scientism is a modern philosophy. Scientism is not Buddhistic because it is the attempt to make the restrictive rules of science into the dogmas by which the whole of life should be governed. Scientism is a different religion and a rather narrow one and it would be a tragedy if Buddhism in the West were reduced to it. Actually, scientism as one finds it in ordinary members of the public is largely based on a version of science that was superseded in the early decades of the twentieth century. I have met people of this persuasion who say that "One should not believe anything that science has not proved." Fortunately or unfortunately, we have discovered that proving is not something that science does. Sometimes science disproves, but science always has an open frontier: it is always open to the new case that overturns what has been thought to be true up to now. Science demonstrates, but such demonstrations are never ultimate or final. We have seen so many revolutions in science in the past century that nobody should be in doubt of this. It does not make science redundant that its findings are so often overturned. It is in the nature of the situation. Science implies that there must be an incalculable amount that we do not know. In this respect science is Buddhistic. Scientism, however, seeks to restrict our vision of the universe to things that are physically demonstrable. Most of the things that are important to most people – love, loyalty, faith, goodness, meaning, purpose - do not fall into such a category. As a philosophy, therefore, scientism is limited. It's popularity is based on a misreading of the prestige that currently attaches to technology. The proposition that one should believe nothing that is not empirically demonstrable is itself not empirically demonstrable.

The Core of Buddhism is a Religious Act

An extension of the popularity of scientistic ways of thinking has become the way that many people currently approach Buddhism as though it were a collection of techniques. Certainly Buddhism has generated many techniques. This is another of its richnesses, but the tendency to see it as being merely technique, or merely practice, is a function of the modern world's worship of technology, not a true representation of Buddhism. It is just another case of picking the fruit while not seeing the root.

We will return to look at some of these technical approaches later. Here, however, we can notice that it is not just Buddhism that has suffered from this tendency. Yoga, for instance, is a religious practice whose purpose in its original setting in Hindu India is the achievement of unification with God. The very term "yoga" refers to such unification, linking or yoking. It is about yoking the individual soul to the godhead until such time as they completely re-merge. Such is the Hindu vision of the meaning of life. In the modern West, yoga is often reduced to a popular form of keep fit. This reductionism is surely a kind of philistinism. Stretching your body into unnatural poses may or may not be good for your joints and muscles, but that is not what yoga was supposed to be all about. Buddhism is in danger of going the same way.

Buddhism is a religion. The common ground - perhaps the only one - of all schools of Buddhism is a religious act called taking refuge. We take refuge in the Three Treasures, Buddha, Dharma and Sangha. Buddha is the supreme source of teaching, love, compassion, and wisdom. Dharma indicates the fundamentals of life and being. Sangha, in this context, is the assembly of spiritually awakened beings. Taking refuge in these three has salvific power. The popular view is that the aim here is to join the

Sangha, learn the Dharma and thereby become a Buddha. That, however, is not refuge. Refuge is not about taking these jewels in our hands, it is about ourselves being held by them.

The spiritual pathway is a succession of deepenings of this act of refuge. Each of these is an awakening of faith. Refuge is the yoga of Buddhism. It is the way that an individual is yoked to the higher meaning and transpersonal evolution of life. It is the way in which the aid of the Buddhas and ancestors is invoked. The mystique of this act is not something that can be grounded in materialism or psychology. It has material and psychological consequences, but they are incidental. The whole purpose is to transcend such considerations and open the possibility of being liberated from them.

Each deepening of refuge is a lessening of ego. More faith, less ego. Thus Buddhism finds salvation beyond self. It is not a collection of methods for greater self-development, self-assertion, self-cherishing, self-esteem, or anything of the kind. Rather the opposite. Buddhism is not narcissism. The devotee is encouraged to be ever mindful of the objects of refuge, to bow to them, make offerings, revere and worship them. Being mindful of their supreme qualities one becomes more aware of one's own deficiency. Becoming more aware of the deficiency of self, one's need to take refuge increases in intensity. Finally one lets go of self entirely, takes refuge wholeheartedly and enters nirvana. Entering nirvana one has faith in the Unborn, the Unconditioned, the Unmade, the Deathless. Having such faith one can live a wholehearted life, uncorrupted by small-mindedness and selfishness.

Along this path, one is led to a deeper enquiry into one's own being with all its limitation, fallibility, weakness, vulnerability and waywardness of passion. The more clearly one is aware of these deficiencies the more in need of refuge one realises oneself to be. One examines the deficiencies of worldly life, the limitations of reason and of the secular world and there arises a distaste for any primary reliance upon them. If that were all, it would be a path to depression and despair. It is not. Buddhists are notably joyful and light of heart. Why so? Because they have faith in a true refuge beyond.

Taking refuge is an act of faith. There is no meaning in taking refuge in a human body that rotted away in India more than two thousand years ago. For a person who takes refuge, Buddha is a deeply treasured presence, otherwise the act is nothing. To think that taking refuge is just like joining a worldly organisation is to miss the essence and to reduce the supreme mystery to a mundane procedure. Far from reducing mystery to mundanity, Buddhism is about infusing the mundane with the sacred.

Buddhists do not claim to explain this presence in terms understandable within the frame of science or materialist common sense. That is precisely the point. It is a question of religion, not of physics - of faith, not chemistry. Religion is concerned with mysteries. These mysteries are supremely important. The idea of disenchanting the world and destroying all its mysteries was an ideal of some nineteenth century intellectuals that has slowly percolated into society and is now widely held by ordinary people who do not fully see the implications. It is a recipe for alienation from the core of life. In any case, it is not Buddhism. The Founder deliberately preserved the status of a Buddha after his demise as a mystery, and so it remains.

Buddhism's foundation is faith. This faith is based in real, close-to-the-bone, experience. We find that the body is not reliable; the mind is not reliable; thoughts are not reliable, emotions are not reliable, circumstances are not reliable, social status is not reliable, the present moment is not reliable. No technique or methodology will make them so. Direct awareness of the present and of the sequence of things occurring demonstrates to us the unreliability of all that the worldly mind considers as self. Awareness alone would leave us frightened and helpless. Therefore we need mindfulness and the other factors of enlightenment that flow from it. We need mindfulness of the treasure that is available to us. Initially we may think it is our own treasure, but this is just the conceit of the self reasserting itself. The treasure is universal and unconditional, but each of us encounters it in a unique way. Buddha speaks to each of us in our own language. Thus everybody has some spiritual treasure to rely upon if they will just heed it. Buddhism helps us to do so with ever greater depth and confidence.

2: How the West has Misunderstood Buddha

Only Some Parts of Some Forms of Buddhism Come West

A few years ago I attended a large international meeting of Buddhists in Tokyo. The vast majority of the three hundred or so people present were from Asian countries. There was a small clutch of North Americans and a scattering of Europeans, myself among them. For the sake of having people who spoke my language I spent some of my time with the Americans. One of the major talking points between them was the absence of meditation from the schedule. One pointed out that on the third day of the event we were all going to go to a big temple nearby. There was general agreement that that must be when we were going to do meditation. The day came. We all went to the temple. It was a magnificent structure. Many Buddhist priests appeared in fine ceremonial robes and an elaborate ritual unfolded. It was beautiful and involved the chanting of scripture and the invocation of Buddhas and holy beings, that they might bring their compassion to our aid. There was no meditation.

This event seemed to me to encapsulate some of what has happened in the translation of Buddhism from East to West. The West already had a faith in technology. Westerners have, therefore, been willing to grasp

Buddhism as a set of techniques. In particular, they have seized upon meditation. Westerners are also rather achievement oriented. Getting results is an important part of our culture. Buddhism has thus been framed as doing meditation in order to get enlightened. Westerners are rather hedonistic. Enlightenment has therefore been interpreted as the end of suffering and finding happiness. Thus Buddhism becomes a personal development programme aimed at the achievement of personal happiness via the practice of meditation.

At the same time, Westerners, or at least the ones that have been attracted by the programme set out in the last paragraph, tend to be resistant to the idea that they are motivated by faith and so they tend not to see the value of rituals that express and foster it. They do not see that their way of practising is itself a ritual that affirms the faith that they have in scientism, nor do they see that this faith is not Buddhist. They hold to the idea that everything needful can be done by the exercise of one's own personal will-power and find ideas of spiritual help coming from outside of themselves unacceptable. The apparent total reliance upon one's own personal resources, which some claim, wrongly, I will argue, to be a hallmark of Buddhism, is something they cherish.

It is common in contemporary discourse to hear assertions such as:

- Buddhism is non-dogmatic
- Zen has no rituals and no priesthood
- Buddhism is not a missionary religion
- Buddhism is non-hierarchical

- Buddha rejected the idea of a supernatural realm and supernatural beings
- there are no metaphysics in Buddhism

All of the above statements are simply wrong. The problem here is that these statements, when made by many Western followers of Buddhism, are not really intended to mean what they say. What they are intended to mean is that Buddhism is not intolerant, persecutory, socially oppressive, or exclusivist and that it does not try to frighten people into conformity by threats of everlasting damnation toward those who dissent. The assertions in the last sentence are, broadly speaking, correct; however, this is not because Buddhism has no dogmas, priests, metaphysics, hierarchies or supernatural beings. Buddhism has all of the latter and still manages to be benign, peace-loving, inclusive, culturally diverse, artistically creative, compassionate and inspiring. How does it do it?

In the Western mind, shaped by Western history, this combination cannot go together. However, any serious examination of Buddhism will show that it can. It follows that for such a serious examination to be maintained, the paradigm that the Western mind is drawing upon has to give way. It is not the case that Buddhism has to be taken to pieces and reconstructed so that it fits into the Western constellation of presumptions. It is, rather, that Buddhism, by its nature, demonstrates that those presumptions are unfounded.

This contemporary attempt at reconstruction is motivated by a desire to keep the presumptions of modernity in place while acknowledging at least some of the fruit of Buddhist civilization. Since modernity says that such riches can only be created by its own reductionist programme, then the undeniable existence of them in Buddhism must mean that Buddhism really and originally must have been some form of modern rationalism and all the huge, diverse plethora of evidence that this is not the case must therefore be a sign of some later cultural overlay that has somehow submerged the original rationalism of the founder. This is a completely false idea. It leads to a kind of mad arrogance. I have heard Westerners visiting Asian countries that have a great depth of Buddhist culture remarking upon how fortunate it is that we in the West have the real Buddhism uncontaminated by all this religious observance that one finds in Asia. This is surely nonsense.

It will be said that as Buddhism has moved from one culture to another in history it has adapted to the new culture. This is half true. When Buddhism went from India to China there ensued a long dialogue, interaction and even struggle between Chinese culture and the new religion. On three major and several other less serious occasions, Buddhism was persecuted as it was seen to represent a serious threat to the paradigm that had previously held sway. In the end, Buddhism adopted some Chinese clothes, but Chinese culture was also substantially remoulded. Initially the Chinese tried to fit Buddhism into frameworks that they already had. At first, most of the terms found in Buddhist texts were matched to terms from Taoism. By around 400 CE, however, it was clear that this was not going to work and the major translations that occurred at that time, especially those of Kumarajiva, in which a vast array of new words were coined, had an impact on Chinese language and culture no less extensive than that of the King James Bible on English.

Heretofore, the West has accepted Buddhism largely on the West's own conditions. We are still in the phase that the Chinese now refer to as that of "matching of terms". If we follow a similar pattern to the impact of Buddhism in China it will not be too long before we start to see that this will not work.

Currently, strident assertions are made that are intended to make Buddhism fit into the existing Western paradigm. However, this is a bit like trying to fit an eagle into a canary cage. Bits stick out all over the place and the truth is that it simply will not all go in. If you were to manage to get it in you would kill it in the process.

The fact that we are still trying to make it fit into too small a cage goes some way toward explaining why the forms of Buddhism that have become popular in the West are often ones that are of minority interest in their countries of origin. We only want those parts that will fit into our cage. In Japan, the Zen schools are far from being the most popular, but in the West they are the form of Japanese Buddhism that has made far and away the greatest progress. In Thailand, the Forest Tradition is a small minority movement of monks who retire to the forest to practice meditation disciplines. The great majority of Thai Buddhists do not follow this approach. Yet it is this form that has become particularly popular in the West.

Nor is the whole of Zen even acceptable. The idea has arisen that Zen has no rituals or clergy, no dogmas or hierarchy, no gods, no soul and so on. However, a Zen temple in Japan generally has many icons that are revered.

Quite commonly Zen temples have no meditation schedule. The standard of faith in Soto Zen, the largest Zen denomination, makes no reference to meditation. In the wake of the recent Fukushima disaster Zen temples in the north of Japan have done a good deal of charitable work helping those who have suffered in the disaster. This work has included extensive practice of exorcisms for the souls of those who now have no descendants to pray for them. Zen operates according to an ecclesial hierarchy with clergy in each village temple who operate much of the time in a manner similar to Christian clergy in Europe. The image that people have of Zen in the West bears little relationship to the reality on the ground in the East.

Nor is Zen a special case. On one occasion, I visited the Jade Buddha Pagoda in Bangkok. This is a big Theravada temple. On arrival, my attention was caught by a large banner hung across the front of the temple with the title in bold English letters "Will Power Institute". I asked the monk who had come to welcome me about the temple. In English, he gave me a well-rehearsed description of Theravada Buddhism as being about self-effort and self-reliance. I asked him if he would show me around. We looked at different rooms in the pagoda. On one of the upper floors was a large room with lines running around the floor. I asked him the purpose and he told me that it was for doing walking meditation. I expressed interest and asked if he would show me how it was done. He willingly assented and showed me how one walks slowly along the lines. The important thing, he explained, was to pray to the Buddha, keep him in mind, call his name and ask for his spiritual power to come into one's life. I commented that this seemed a bit at variance with the idea of self-reliance that he had started with and with the principles of a "Will Power Institute." He smiled disarmingly and said that all that was for the North American visitors who like that kind of thing.

Selective Blindness Screens Out the Main Point

Westerners are inclined to dismiss the devotional, supernatural and metaphysical aspects of Buddhism. There is a kind of selective blindness and deafness at work. If we were to let those elements in it would burst our cage and we don't want that. It is as if, when asked to describe a rainbow, one said that it was red and yellow and, when asked if there were not other colours, one said that the other colours are not real, just distortions of the red and yellow added afterwards. However, it is doubtful if a person who can only see red and yellow can really grasp what a rainbow is. Reading a Buddhist text, the Westerner seems not to notice the references to rebirth, to conversations with deities, to supernatural occurrences, to faith, to past aeons, to celestial Buddhas, and to anything else that does not fit into the modernist paradigm. However, if we look carefully we should be able to see that the modernist paradigm is just a paradigm, just as there have been plenty of others over the history of humanity and, no doubt, will be others to come. Buddhism too has its paradigm. To understand a path one must at least suspend doubt about the paradigm within which that path is located. One must allow one's cage to be rattled.

This blindness or limitedness also affects how Buddhist texts get translated into Western languages. Buddhism has a great deal of distinctive terminology and in many cases the terms are defined by reference to one another. If you change the translation of a few key terms the knock-on effect can be to change the whole meaning of the philosophy. This is not just a Western problem. Buddhist texts have been translated many times in the course of history and it is doubtful if we have any of what the founder, Shakyamuni, actually said in its original form, even though we have a huge amount in translation. Fortunately the languages of India are often rather similar to one another so the early translations may not have been too bad. When it came to translation into Tibetan or Chinese, however, the technical problems were considerable, quite apart from the distortions that enter in due to the personal preferences or degree of insight of the translator.

It has become standard practice to translate many Buddhist terms into English by using English words that sound rather scientific, like form, perception, consciousness and so on. These terms are mostly value neutral. However, the texts in which the original terms are found were polemics. The Buddha was not trying to give a scientific, neutral account of how the mind works. He was advocating a change of outlook. It has become common to assert that Buddhism is non-judgemental and does not differentiate between different positions. The Buddha himself, however, never shrinks from distinguishing the views of "those ordinary people who have no regard for noble ones and are unskilled and undisciplined in Dharma" from those of true disciples who are "accomplished and fully enlightened". When commenting on the practice of bathing in the holy rivers of India, which was commonly believed to be a means of purification, he says "A fool may bathe there forever yet not purify wrong

deeds." (MN7.20) Buddha was not shy of distinguishing his position from that of other teachers and the language that he used was often loaded with value implications and even sarcasm.

An effect of this mode of translation, no doubt intended to make Buddhism sound more scientific, is sometimes to create statements that are complete nonsense. Thus, for instance, the term *vijnana* is now standardly translated as "consciousness" even though it is clear in many texts that it refers to something that the Buddha advocated overcoming and getting rid of. Do we really think that the Buddha advocated as a goal to arrive at a state where there is no consciousness? A similar issue arises with the translation of *vedana* as "feeling". Is Buddhism really aimed at a life without feelings? Some have come to think so, but this is surely a mistake. If we translate the words that Buddha used to designate the aspects of life that hold us from spiritual awakening into English terms that refer to factors present in the life of every living human being, we create a text in translation that, in effect, says that spiritual awakening is not possible for a real human being. It is obvious that this was not the Buddha's original intended meaning, but one can see how it emerges from the desire to make Buddhism look and sound dispassionately scientific.

It also has another, more subtle, effect. By creating statements that advocate aims that are not attainable by a living human being, it puts would-be practitioners in a double bind. This leads to people striving for years to attain something that is not attainable and, in the process, missing the more straightforward meaning that could put their life on a sounder footing.

It is, perhaps, ironic that Buddhism should suffer from the effects of such selective blindness, because it was selective blindness (*avidya*) that Buddha saw as a key element in human conceit and delusion. The whole purpose of Buddhism could be seen as being to burst our cages. Be that as it may, the fact that Buddha gave avidya such an important role has led many to think that he was a rationalist who favoured "enlightenment", rather in the sense that that term had in Europe and America in the eighteenth and nineteenth centuries, namely a worship of consciousness and abandonment of everything that they considered irrational. The problem here is that much of the Buddha's teaching is in the form of showing the disadvantages of such blindness rather than in specifying what it was that the blindness was missing. This has led Westerners to miss the Buddha's positive message which was often more implied than spelt out.

The paradigm of modernity is largely based on the metaphor of a mechanism. We feel that we have explained something when we have shown what kind of mechanism it is and how that mechanism works. Psychology has, to a considerable extent, grown up as an attempt to explain people as mechanisms. When mechanisms break down they can be fixed by a mechanic. Psychotherapy is often presented as a kind of mechanics of the soul. We try to identify syndromes of supposed mental disease and match to them treatments or remedies that, in principle, could be universally administered by anybody who correctly diagnosed the problem and then followed the instructions. Actually, life is not like that. When Buddha met the mad woman Patacara, or the killer, Angulimala, or the bereaved mother, Kisagotami, he did not cure any of them by administering a pre-formulated procedure. Nor, if any of these people had met somebody other than the Buddha, would the effect have been the same even if the person they met had said exactly the same things to them as Buddha did. Encounters that inspire faith cannot be reduced to a formula.

Nonetheless, we have tended to apply the same approach to Buddhism. It gets analysed into methods and doctrines and these are taken to constitute an instruction manual for fixing the human soul, curing neurosis and spiritual blindness, and achieving smooth running of the supposed human mechanism. Ironically this "instruction manual" approach has, as one of its by-products, a reading of Buddhism as more dogmatic than it actually is. Western adherents cling tenaciously to strings of creedal or imperative statements such as:

- everything is impermanent
- achieve non-dual awareness
- everything is suffering
- live in the here and now
- practise detachment
- everything inter-exists with everything else

... and so forth, that, while not wholly erroneous, are, nonetheless, being held to in a distinctly un-Buddhist manner.

I recently had a book published called *Not Everything is Impermanent*. When I show this book to Western Buddhists they do not understand. I am likely to get comments such as "But I thought that Buddhism teaches that everything is impermanent," or "How can there be anything that is not impermanent?" This, from people who believe that they are being non-dogmatic. However, when I show the book to Buddhists in Asia, I am much more likely to get such responses as, "Ah, yes, nirvana," or, simply, "Of course." The point here is that Asian Buddhists tend to understand that when Buddha talked about the unsatisfactoriness of impermanence, he was telling people that taking refuge in ephemeral things such as social standing, possessions, status and the like was insecure and so they should seek a more reliable refuge, whereas Western Buddhists simply think that Buddha was making an ontological statement about the nature of the world and getting us used to the idea that there is nothing more reliable. They take it as disenchanting and reductionist; they do not see the spiritual or liberationist implication.

The Asian Buddhists are, in this comparison, surely correct. Buddha was not interested in telling people about ontology. He was interested in their spiritual salvation. Buddha said that if there were nothing that was not impermanent then there could be no liberation or salvation (Udana 8), and he clearly did not believe that to be the case. The whole point of Buddhism is that as life in the conditioned world is unsatisfactory one should take refuge in the unconditioned. Technically, "the unconditioned" cannot really be classified as anything other than a metaphysical dogma, and it is this that is the basis of salvation in Buddhism. This is not a problem from the Buddhist perspective because Buddhism is a religion. It is only a problem from the modernist, reductionist position that cannot cope with anything that goes beyond the physical.

3: Buddhism is Metaphysical

Metaphysics Got a Bad Name

The term “metaphysics” derives from the works of Aristotle. He himself called it “first philosophy”. It is concerned with the ultimate and/or original nature, purpose, meaning and relations of things. The word means what comes after physics. Physics originally meant nature. So metaphysics is our attempt to explain our nature and the nature of what we encounter. Metaphysics thus includes theology as well as questions about what is not impermanent, not conditional, not merely relative.

One fundamental difference between Buddhism and modernity lies in the attempt of modernity to do away with metaphysics. This venture started in the eighteenth century and gathered momentum in the nineteenth when it seemed possible, probable even, that a completely rational systematic understanding of the natural universe was going to be possible. Mathematics was going to provide a watertight system of logic, completely free from internal contradiction, physics was going to explain all the forces in the universe, chemistry was going to reduce life, love, thought and meaning to epiphenomena of the movements of elementary, irreducible particles. Such was the positivistic vision. There was no need or place in it for metaphysical considerations. God, grace, spirit, genius and soul were to become unnecessary hypotheses.

Shakespeare's opus was going to be shown to be a mere epiphenomenon of atomic particles moving in a completely deterministic manner. Some people still think this way.

It takes a century or two for the enthusiasm of cutting edge intellectuals to percolate into popular consciousness and become "common sense", so our culture is currently in the undertow or backwash of that gloriously misguided enthusiasm that gripped the best minds of Europe two hundred years ago. The twentieth century, however, dawned with Bertrand Russell pointing out an irresolvable conundrum in the most foundational theory of mathematics and Sigmund Freud publishing his iconoclastic work on the fathoming of dreams. This shaking of the foundations of positivism continued with the splitting of the elementary particles, Einstein's $e=mc^2$, the uncertainty principle, and all the cosmological speculations that have now put us in a position where the universe is once again a profound mystery. This will not become common sense in our generation. However, it has led to modernism giving way, to some extent, to postmodernism, which is really a kind of salvaging operation, attempting to retain as much as possible of the positivistic vision in circumstances in which all its original hopes appear to be completely out of reach and ill-founded.

These are the philosophical circumstances in which Buddhism has come west. Not surprisingly it has been hijacked by some in support of a modernist agenda and by others, a postmodernist one. However, Buddhism is neither of these and its use to prop up these occidental positions inevitably involves a very selective reading and even some outright distortion. In particular, the whole metaphysical project of Buddhism tends to get willfully overlooked since the need for such a project is exactly what modernists and post-modernists do not see.

This is possible in the case of Buddhism because frequently Buddhist texts reveal their metaphysical content indirectly, which is to say, by a process of negating the physical rather than asserting metaphysical propositions directly. Thus, that whole section of Buddhist wisdom called the *Prajna Paramita* is replete with statements such as: “No eye, no ear, no nose, no tongue, no body, no mind; no visual object, no audible object, no olfactory object, no object of taste, no tactile object, no object of mind.” So, none of these... what then? *Prajna paramita* literally means “discerning the other shore”, the other shore being the spiritual domain, which is, surely, a metaphysical project. The general import is that the metaphysical is critically more important than the merely physical or empirical.

The West has lost faith in metaphysics because of a belief that some metaphysical propositions have been discredited. However, scientific propositions regularly get discredited and we do not lose faith in science. If all the currently held theories about gravitation, electromagnetism and the dynamics of physical bodies were, in due course, to be discredited, as they may well be, this would not discredit physics as such. The same should be true with metaphysics. It is a project with an open frontier. That certain propositions fall into disuse or seem counterproductive does not discredit the project as a whole. It is the transaction between the physical and the metaphysical that is the driving force of life. That both are endlessly revealing themselves in new ways does not negate this fundamental.

The modernist project was driven by a revulsion for the kind of metaphysical position-taking that had had disastrous consequences in European history. Hair-splitting distinctions in opinions about the ways in which the metaphysical domain should be described, defined and celebrated had become the pretext for wars, persecutions and cruelty. No wonder there was a reaction. We could say that the reaction has been so strong that it amounted to a case of throwing out the baby with the bath water.

Buddhism did not have such a history to contend with. Although metaphysical issues have perennially been a matter of debate in Buddhism, such debate has rarely been the cause of social disorder or persecution. Valuing the metaphysical rather than the physical has, rather, been the basis of the Buddhist advocacy and practice of simplicity, poverty, non-violence and renunciation.

Humans are creatures of language. Words, on the one hand, signify physical objects, but, on the other hand, signify meanings that transcend particular objects. In any case, many of the objects of language are abstract or conventional rather than physical. We live in a physical world, but we cannot help doing so by abstract and metaphysical means. To deny metaphysics as such simply leaves people living in a meaningless universe and many, nowadays, do feel alienated in precisely this way.

Buddhism, on the other hand, is pre-eminently metaphysical. It is the meaning and purpose that are important and the physical circumstances that are incidental. The person of faith and awakening is able to navigate an infinite variety of physical circumstances without losing their metaphysical bearings. This does not mean that Buddhism is an unbending system of metaphysical ideas rigidly held. It means, rather, that the spiritual life is one in which one becomes at ease with seeing and exploring the deeper meaning rather than just being taken in by surface appearance. In Buddhism, metaphysics is an alive activity, not a dead system.

Not only is Buddhism metaphysical; for Buddhists, Buddha is metaphysical. The Western Buddhist likes to emphasise that "Buddha never claimed to be a god" with a view to stripping the Buddha of any metaphysical pretension. However, Buddha is presented by Buddhists as the teacher of the gods, which hardly bears out this reductionist contention. In fact, for Buddhists, Buddha is an eternally continuing presence in metaphysical form. In the doctrine of the Three Body (*trikaya*) nature of Buddha, all three bodies are essentially metaphysical.

Western Buddhist temples like to have a statue of Shakyamuni as their centrepiece. This enables them to talk about the historical Buddha and to spend time reassuring each other that Buddhism is simply a matter of facts that happened in history. East Asian temples rarely have Shakyamuni as their centrepiece. For them it is not history or facticity that matter. It is the spiritual meaning. The Buddhas that are enshrined are metaphysical. They exist in other dimensions and other worlds. They are Quan Shi Yin, the holy being of compassion, Manjushri, the holy being of wisdom, Samantabhadra, the all-good one, and innumerable others. Probably the most popular is Amitabha, the Buddha of measureless light. Asian Buddhists want to live in this measureless light. History is incidental.

Is this just a difference of style between East and West, or does it run deeper? I suggest that by endlessly re-emphasising facticity, the concrete, the historical, and the psychological we run the danger of blocking our own access to the heart of the matter. We are trying to cut Buddhism down to a size we are familiar with when what is needed is that we grow into the bigger-mindedness and bigger-heartedness that it is offering us. We are like people who never learn to swim because they will not let go of the rail on the edge of the pool.

Metaphysical Communication

The trikaya doctrine that has just been mentioned is open to a variety of interpretations. I will give one here, but do not take this as the final or authoritative word on the subject. In the West we are used to metaphysics being an area in which hard positions are defended and battle lines are drawn. Buddhism is more fluid. The metaphysical dimension is all important, but you must explore it for yourself. Doctrines are useful in the way that maps are useful. They are never complete or final, but they have utility. Some maps are more detailed than others and some are more accurate than others, but the activity that matters is to use whatever map one has got in order to navigate and explore so that one has a direct experience of the territory. Also, you are allowed to write your own notes on the map and you might have your own idiosyncratic names for some of the features you encounter as you go along. To argue, or worse, fight, over which map is best, or what a particular feature should be called, is little more than a distraction and prevarication, and, in any case, in Buddhism, would be regarded as bad form.

So the trikaya, or three body, teaching is a useful metaphysical map. Not all Buddhists use it, but many do. There are also two body versions. However, I think it is accurate to say that virtually all Asian Buddhists do have some idea of the Buddha as a metaphysical presence in their lives, not merely as a man who died a long time ago.

I said I would give an elucidation of the trikaya nature, so here goes. Buddha's metaphysical nature can be understood as having three manifestations. The ultimate or fundamental of these is called the *Dharmakaya*. *Kaya* means body. The word *dharma* gets translated in many ways in Western renderings of Buddhist texts and you can read that it has many meanings. My preference, however, is to take it as meaning "the fundamental". Buddha-Dharma is Buddha's fundamental teaching, or, we could say, Buddha's teaching on what is fundamental, or, even, Buddha as fundamental. Buddha-Dharma is the religion in which Buddha is fundamental. The myriad dharmas are the innumerable fundamental things or units of existence. The Dharmakaya is the fundamental body, and it is the most metaphysical. Consequently, almost whatever we try to say about it is going to be too limiting. The Dharmakaya is the unconditional love, compassion, truth and being of Buddha that pervades all existence – yet even this description is too restricting. Let's just stay with the idea that the ultimate nature of Buddha, Dharmakaya, is so totally metaphysical that one cannot fully grasp it this side of complete spiritual awakening.

The great medieval writer on Zen, Eihei Dogen, has this to say about it:

The true Dharmakaya of Buddha
Is like space.
Its manifestations accord with the forms of things
As those of the moon in water.
~ Dogen in the chapter Tsuki in Shobogenzo

So the Dharmakaya is in one sense ungraspable, while, nonetheless, being omnipresent. Nothing could be more metaphysical than that. That being so, Buddha's limitless compassion also flowers in two further manifestations that are relatively more accessible to the ordinary person. These are called the *sambhogakaya* and the *nirmanakaya*. They are, as it were, aspects of Dharmakaya. They are the moon in the water whereas Dharmakaya is the moonlight itself. I've used a capital initial for Dharmakaya to emphasise its importance, but there are no capitals in Sanskrit. These Sanskrit words, *sambhogakaya* and *nirmanakaya*, mean "enjoyment bodies" and "transformation bodies" respectively. I have put the terms in the plural because they each can have a limitless diversity of forms. This limitless diversity is possible because these are terms for things that are metaphysical, not physical.

Enjoyment bodies are how Buddhas appear in the course of spiritual experience. When we see visions or dream dreams, a Buddha may appear to us and communicate with us. This will be a sambhogakaya-buddha. There are many sambhogakaya-buddhas. They are often associated with particular Buddha qualities:

Quan Yin with compassion, Manjushri with wisdom, and so on. Being metaphysical, we do not need to concern ourselves too obsessively with the boundaries between one and another, or get caught up in questions of historical origins. What is at stake is the manner in which spiritual wisdom is conveyed to the devotee. Many of the great figures of Buddhist history did what they did because of the appearance to them of a sambhogakaya-buddha who gave them an important instruction at a critical time. In some ways, sambhogakaya-buddhas are angels. The term angel means a messenger who brings something from the spiritual domain to we who dwell in the mundane world. Thus Atisha, who is one of the pivotal figures in the establishment of Tibetan Buddhism, was one day in his home country of Bengal when a sambhogakaya-buddha appeared to him and told him to go and travel to Indonesia where he would find a teacher called Selingpa. It was from Selingpa that Atisha receivedt the important teachings that he was later to take to Tibet. Thus too, Shinran, now regarded as the founder of what has become the largest school of Buddhism in Japan, was nearing the end of a one hundred day retreat when a sambhogakaya-buddha appeared to him and told him to go and seek teachings from the, at that time unconventional and controversial teacher, Honen Shonin. Thus began one of the most fertile transmissions of the Dharma.

The Western person reading this will commonly be inclined to start trying to think of other ways in which these occurrences can be explained, or, we might even say, explained away. The Western educated person wants to explain them away in order to maintain intact the current positivistic, reductionistic paradigm. Of course, that paradigm has developed various lines of argument for the purpose of explaining away this kind of phenomenon. It would, wouldn't it? Whether you regard such arguments as convincing or contrived is probably more a matter of taste than logic. The point is, however, that Buddhism is not part of that paradigm. The Buddhist way of regarding spiritual occurrences is... well, spiritual, and that is that. At face value, Buddhas do appear and tell people what to do and when they do it there can be some extraordinary consequences.

Because Atisha took what the sambhogakaya-buddha said to him in a religious way we today have Tibetan Buddhism and because Shinran did so we have Japanese Buddhism. If they had taken it in the manner prescribed by modernity we would have had neither. Religion moves people to do amazing things.

We still need, for completeness, to say something about the nirmanakaya-buddhas or transformation bodies. This refers to the fact that Buddhas can actually appear in any form whatsoever. The person sitting next to you on the bus might be a Buddha. Sometimes the spiritual world breaks through into this world using the medium of ordinary-seeming people and objects. This would include the fact that Shakyamuni was a human being. All great teachers are nirmanakaya: human beings manifesting Dharma nature.

As I say, those of a materialist bent will now say, "But this is just..." and the "just" reveals the intention to reduce spiritual life to factors that can be accommodated within a materialist framework. The point here is not really to argue that such a perspective is true or false, but rather to make plain that *it is not Buddhism*. Buddhism is not about taking spiritual occurrences and saying that they are just mundane occurrence interpreted a certain way. Buddhism is about believing in the higher meaning of what is happening, the potency of the metaphysical dimension, the inspiring power of non-material beings. Buddhism is a religion.

Buddha was clear about the significance of worship and veneration. For instance, when his life was ending, he told his assistant, Ananda, about the importance of having holy places of pilgrimage:

There are four places, Ananda, that a pious person should visit and regard with sentiments of reverence: The place where the Tathagata was born; the place where the Tathagata became spiritually awakened, the place where the Tathagata set the Wheel of the Dharma in motion, and the place where the Tathagata was finally unbound into ultimate nirvana. These are places that a pious person should visit and regard with sentiments of reverence. And it will come to pass that to these places will come pious monks and nuns, laymen and laywomen, and they will reflect that "This is where the Tathagata was born, here he became spiritually awakened, here he set the Wheel of the Dharma in motion, and here he passed away. (Mahaparinibbana Sutta)

He gave instructions for the dressing and cremating of his body after this death and for the creation of a stupa. A stupa is a mound commemorating a saint or hero. We have already referred to it in the section on Buddhist architecture and the evolution of the pagoda. Why are such monuments important?

Because, Ananda, when they think 'This is the stupa of the Blessed One, the Arhat, the Fully Enlightened,' the hearts of many people will become calm and blissful and, thus made tranquil and full of faith, at the dissolution of the body, after death, they will be reborn in a heavenly realm of happiness.... and, whoever offers flowers or incense and pays homage there and thus pacifies their heart, it will be for their happiness and welfare for a long time. (ibid.)

It is clear from statements of this kind that Buddha recommended devotional religious practices. In fact, it seems probable that for ordinary people, Buddhism was, from the beginning, substantially a matter of stupa worship. Circumambulating the stupa while chanting mantras was probably the most popular form of public collective practice.

4: What is Religion About?

Relating to the Absolute

Many people in the West have turned away from religion and at the same time, in many other parts of the world, religion is becoming a stronger force in world affairs. Turning away from certain specific religions, some have developed a desire to get rid of all religion.

Buddhism is distinctive. In a sense, Buddhism is not so much *a* religion as an investigation into the fundamental nature of religion itself. Now many Western people are interested in such a venture, but they are interested in investigating the nature of religion from a perspective that holds itself outside of religion. In order to maintain this position they adhere to all the conventions and restrictions demanded by academic discipline. The results are interesting, but they are, inevitably, simply academic. That is what they were intended to be. Buddhism, on the other hand, is an investigation of the fundamental (*dharma*) nature of religion undertaken from within. Here religion is being explored from inside, and the exploration takes one deeper and deeper into a religious perspective. Buddhism is the pursuit of the question of what it means to be truly religious: to give oneself wholly and wholeheartedly to meanings and purposes that go far beyond the mundane.

Buddhism is often seen as being less dogmatic than other religions. This is not because Buddhism is wishy-washy or lacks principles. It is because Buddhism seeks to explore religion at the most ultimate and fundamental level which is also the most intimate and personal. Buddhism is looking for the essence of religion, not at arm's length, but by direct and intimate experience. The principles derived from such a search should be applicable to all religions, but the aim is not really to distil principles. Nonetheless, this universality of applicability accounts for the fact that it is not uncommon to come across people who rejected the religion of their childhood, later turned to Buddhism and, much later, through their experience of Buddhism, started to regain an appreciation of what their original religion was all about. Buddhism is not fundamentally in competition with other religions; it speaks the ground of all religion.

This means that Buddhism asserts the central importance of religion in life. It is not a way of negating religion, but of deepening our appreciation that it is the religious consciousness that is at the very core of our being.

The ground of all religion can be thought about in a number of ways. One of these is to say that religion is the way that we creatures of this relative, conditional world relate to the absolute: to the unconditional, unborn, undying, that we cannot help intuiting. Buddha says that to reach the state where one has the unconditioned, which Buddhists call nirvana, always in mind, whether consciously or simply implicitly, is spiritually liberating. It is this relationship between the conditioned and the unconditioned that defines religion, together with the features commonly associated with it: the distinction between revered and mundane objects and people; feelings of awe, wonder, contrition, trust and so on; moral codes; prayers and rituals; a spiritual community bound together by such values; and a sense of the supreme importance of this understanding that makes it possible for some people to entirely centre their lives upon it. Religions are concerned with life and death and their meaning. This focus inevitably creates a distinction between concerns in terms of their significance in relation to ultimate meaning. When you are dying you will not be worrying about how to pay the rent or whether to buy a new car. The miracle of life and death is a much bigger affair.

Our Fundamental Intuition

There are important things in our life which we only know by intuition. Intuition is not necessarily vague; it can be very precise and specific. We might try to be rational and calculating in life, but, in reality, most of our most important decisions, such as who to marry, where to live, what to choose as one's life's work, are made by intuition; and if they are not made by intuition then they are suspect. The person who marries for money, or some other similar calculation, is living in a way that we all immediately, and intuitively, recognise as unsatisfactory.

To understand religion, we have to rehabilitate the role of intuition in our lives. Intuition is the compass of spirit. Without it we are lost upon a materialistic ocean that offers no reliable clues about direction. Rational calculation can sometimes tell us how best to accomplish something, but it cannot tell us what to try to accomplish, or, if it does, as when we dedicate our lives to accumulating more and more physical objects, then it trivialises our existence.

What do I mean by such intuition? Isn't our experience simply limited to this empirical world? No, it isn't. We all know how to count. One, two, three, four.... We know these are numbers, but what is a number? Does a number exist in the empirical world? No. The nature of numbers is a puzzle. Newton's famous book *Principia Mathematica* takes more than 300 pages defining the number “1”. Let's go further, much further. What is the biggest number? In the empirical world there is always a biggest, just as there is always a smallest. If you have a group of ten children you can see who is tallest. Even of all the people in the world, there must be one who is tallest. This is because the number of people is always finite. Numbers however just go on and on. There can always be a bigger one. We never encounter numbers as such and even if we could we could never encounter the biggest one. We intuit something called infinity. Infinity is an absolute. It does not exist in the empirical world. In empirical mathematics you are forbidden to speak of infinity. However, we can all intuit the idea of infinity even though we never meet it in real life. Mr Infinity never knocks on our door, yet, somehow, we already know him well. Even in supposedly empirical mathematics we have to accommodate “irrational numbers”, “unreal numbers”, functions that never converge, and many other strange beasts that one will never encounter on the street.

Furthermore, infinity does not behave like other numbers we have met. Three plus three is six. Six is bigger than three. Infinity plus a trillion is still just infinity. Half of infinity is still infinity. The absolute is not subject to the same rules as the world of relative measurement. We seem to be able to accept this in the domain of maths, yet have difficulty seeing that it applies to all the other absolute ultimates that we navigate our life by. however, goodness is always good. A small good act is goodness. A big good act is goodness. Goodness is always goodness whether it is implemented in a small way or a big way, or even if it remains in the heart, as yet unimplemented. *It is possible to say that goodness does not exist and infinity does not exist and so on, but what an impoverishment of life that would be!* In any case, it would be rather artificial to impose a rule upon ourselves that we must not make use of intuitions that we all have that have been vitally useful to humanity throughout its history. The attempt to do away with metaphysics has left contemporary people impoverished in that way, alienated, reduced and lacking a sense of anything ultimate, anything beyond physics. That is not Buddhism. Buddhism is about relating to the unconditioned. Buddha said so.

So, religion is how we relate to absolute truth. Anything absolute, like infinity, is a mystery to us, but just because it is mysterious does not mean that it is not relevant, nor does it mean that thinking about it cannot be rigorous. Life itself is a mystery and the absolute mystery is the way we make sense of it, insofar as we do. Sense comes from context and ultimate sense comes from ultimate context.

We live in a relative world, yet we can intuit what is absolute. Or, to say the same thing a different way, we live in a world of phenomena, but we intuit a world of noumena. In our hearts and minds we inhabit two domains, the phenomenal and the noumenal. This has something to do with the nature of language. I cannot be too specific because this is a subject that philosophers have debated for millennia, but I will try to convey the general idea. We encounter something in the world and we have a name for it. Let's use the example of a mountain. There is the mountain in the distance. We know about it as an empirical entity. We can approach it, walk round it, climb on it. We, therefore, say that it is real, because it impinges on our experience.

However, when we say that it is a mountain, the word mountain does not merely signify this particular mountain. This particular mountain is a phenomenon. However, when we say that it is *a* mountain we are aggregating it to a category. We know of other mountains. The word mountain does not actually exactly specify any of them particularly. Rather we have an idea of mountain-ness. Philosophers argue over whether this idea of mountain-ness has been derived from actual mountains or is derived from something deeper, more instinctual or archetypal in us. Is it the case that we make the idea of mountain-ness by a process of abstraction from a series of experiences of particular mountains, or is the potential to understand mountain-ness in a certain way something that is already inherent in us before we ever see a specific mountain? For our purposes here, it does not matter. What matters is that there is a domain of actual mountains that are empirical phenomena in our world and there is a domain of ideas of mountain-ness, table-ness, tree-ness and so on that are, in a sense, more perfect than the phenomenal objects. These ideas are beyond the physical objects which means that they are meta-physical. Whether the metaphysical or the physical come first is a matter for philosophers to puzzle over. All we need to acknowledge here is that both domains are important to us. I am not here wishing to assert or deny the ideas of the philosopher Plato, simply to make clear that even when we think we are being empirical, we are all the time using abstract ideas in order to do so.

We have a capacity to access a world of ideas that constitute a more perfect world than the one we actually inhabit. In fact, this is more than just a capacity. The idea of capacity implies it is something we can switch on and off, but what we are talking about here is so much a part of what it is to be human that we do not have the option to switch it off. The intuited perfect or absolute domain constantly accompanies us in all our actual phenomenal experience. Without it we could not make sense of our world. We are constantly in the business of aggregating actual experiences by reference to our intuition of the absolute.

This is also the genesis of our sense of ideals. We have ideals inasmuch as we have a sense that the actual ought to be more like the absolute than it actually is. We want the mountain to be a perfect mountain. We want each thing to be a perfect instance of what it is, but the "perfect" case is not actually an instance at all, the perfect case is the absolute idea which does not form part of the empirical world. Nonetheless, the absolute domain plays a vitally important part in our life. Without it we would have no ideals and hence no sense of direction or meaning. We actually function as if the metaphysical is more real than the physical. The metaphysical impacts upon us.

Thus, for instance, the love that we actually encounter in this world is always in some degree and in some manner conditional, yet from our experience of such love we intuitively conceive of unconditional love. The absolute domain is unconditional. Unconditionality makes complete sense to us even though we never encounter it empirically. Such a reality as unconditional love is something that is of great importance to us even though it is not part of our physical world. It is metaphysical. Religion is about how we relate to such metaphysical fundamentals. Religious practices help us to understand them and keep them in mind and, most importantly, revere them. They should be revered because their power over us is great.

For Buddhists, Buddha is such a metaphysical entity. Dharma is another. Buddhists revere them. People in the grip of secularism attempt to strip Buddha and Dharma of their aura of sanctity and suggest that reverence has no place in the new, bold rational universe that they want to create. Such a soulless world, however, is not human and not desirable. Nonetheless, even that ideal is a metaphysical idea.

The idea that one should only believe in what one encounters empirically is impractical. People are simply not made that way. Life is a constant interaction between the physical and the metaphysical. Those who want to abolish the latter from consideration are deceiving themselves. Actually, most such people believe in a concept that they have of science. The concept "science" is itself a metaphysical idea. The sciences we encounter in the empirical world are never as pure as the ones that exist in our intuition. Further, science is an art of relating measurements to one another. Measurements are abstractions. A measurement is not a phenomenon in the way that a chair is. You can sit on a chair. You cannot sit on a measurement. A bird could land on a chair. The bird would never see, hear or smell any of these measurements that we put such store by. Science is not really concerned with real things so much as with measurements derived from real things. All these measurements are ideas. In Buddhist terms, they are rupas, not dharmas. Rupas are forms that have some power over our mind. Dharmas are the fundamental things in themselves.

You can measure the height of a mountain. You can then say that this mountain is taller than that mountain and not so high as the other one. However, the mountain is a mountain, it is not a height. By knowing the height we know something *about* the mountain, but we do not know the mountain.

We could pursue these ideas much, much further. Philosophers have been doing so for centuries. Whatever detailed view one takes of the nature of abstraction, ideas, the absolute, the noumenal, the metaphysical, the fact remains that we occupy two domains at the same time and we are constantly relating one to the other and the other to the one, and it is from the metaphysical domain that we derive our ideals and, therefore, much of our motivation in life.

The Buddha was called a *lokavid. Loka* means world or domain. *Vid* we have in English in such terms as video. It means "to see". The Buddha was called lokavid because he could see both of these worlds clearly and the relation between them. This is one way of understanding what Buddhism is. Buddhism is awakening to these two domains. It is being able to live a life that is as fully physical and as fully metaphysical as possible. The metaphysical is implemented in the physical and the physical becomes meaningful through the metaphysical. Such is human life.

In Buddhism, the metaphysical domain is called the other shore (*paramita*). It is a domain that, in itself, is completely empty (*shunya*) of anything empirical – no form, no sound, no taste, no smell, no touch, and not even imaginary objects. This empti-ness (*shunya-ta*) is timeless. It is a domain that is not subject to impermanence. Even if my ideas about these matters are inaccurate in detail, there is no getting away from the fact that our intuition of a noumenal world, however we conceive it, is important. That we struggle with understanding it is only natural, but to try to banish it is not going to work.

Wholly within the phenomenal world, that dharma over there cannot really be said to be "mountain". The that-ness (*tatha-ta*) of that dharma over there is ungraspable in words. The same is true on the other side (*paramita*). Wholly within the shunyata domain there cannot really be said to be specific ideas, for what is absolute is also ungraspable. Human life is conducted on a bridge between two domains that for the ordinary person remain both mostly out of sight. They might be out of sight, but they do not have to be out of mind. Buddhism advocates keeping them in mind. This is what mindfulness means and such mindfulness is the first factor of enlightenment. It permits the further investigation of dharmas and that, in turn, supports all the virtues that constitute the awakened state.

All this is of overwhelming importance for the conduct of our actual lives, whether we realise it or not.

However, insofar as we do realise it and keep it in mind we find we have a much more reliable compass for our lives. Life occurs in a continually swirling dynamic as the physical and metaphysical aspects interpenetrate. To keep the unborn in mind is like keeping the pole star in view. You cannot go there, but you can navigate by it.

Let me try to summarise a few points made so far. Religion is how we relate to the absolute. We intuit the absolute, the unconditional, noumenal from the relative, conditional, phenomenal. We make sense of the phenomenal by reference to the noumenal, the physical by reference to the metaphysical. The ultimately empirical and the ultimately noumenal are not graspable with words, but they are real intuitions of great moment to our actual lives. Life is lived in the in-between. In that in-between, out of the metaphysical we crystallise ideals, values, and motives and out of the physical we abstract measurements and methods for putting these ideals into practice. This activity of value formation and implementation constitutes our spiritual life, or, we could say, the spirit of our life.

The Spirit of Our Life

A flower is a physical object. Joe takes some flowers home from work to give to his wife. Mary thus obtains some physical objects. Some physical objects pass from one person to another. This is what happens in the physical world. Another day, Joe takes home a piece of cow dung. He gives it to Mary. Mary obtains another physical object. If we confine ourselves to the physical reality we do not understand much.

The important things in our lives are not the physical objects. The important things lie in the area of meaning, which is to say, spirit or heart. In the West we say spirit, in the East they say heart. In what spirit does Joe give Mary the flowers? This is what matters. Perhaps the flowers are a gesture of appreciation and love; perhaps they are a peace offering; perhaps they are a bribe; perhaps Joe paid a lot of money for the flowers; perhaps he stole them. These options define different spiritual possibilities.

At the purely physical level Mary gains an object and Joe loses one. If, however, it is a love token, Joe does not lose. A loving gift is a gain to both giver and receiver. A bribe, on the other hand, may be a loss to both. Gain and loss at the spiritual level are not the same as gain and loss at the physical level.

When Mary receives the piece of cow dung she is probably not as joyful as when she receives the flowers. This is assuming that the scene is somewhere in modern suburbia. Were it in an African village where cow dung was an essential fuel, the response might be different. It is not the object, it is the meaning, and the meaning derives from the spirit of the act. Our lives are spiritual.

The spiritual is the bridge between the absolute and the physical, between the metaphysical and the physical. The physical token is only appreciated inasmuch as it speaks of the metaphysical fundamental.

We act in the physical world according to a spirit derived from our relationship to the absolute. Whether a person considers him or herself to be a spiritual person or not, the feelings that they have in life are a function of how they discern the spirit of the acts that they perform and that are performed by those close to them and by others toward them. It is the spirit that matters. The less able one is to appreciate the spirit of things the more grasping and fearful one is likely to be and the less capable one will be of participating in the kind of subtle transactions between people that make life noble, meaningful and satisfying.

So, to recapitulate, at the spiritual level there is a different calculus from at the physical level. At the physical level one person gains and another loses. However, at the spiritual level if it is a sincere gift, both gain, if it is a theft, the receiver loses, if it is a bribe, both lose, and so on. What is the nature of the gain? It is an increase in love, faith, and morale. What is the nature of the loss? It is corruption.

Buddhism is concerned with this calculus. Buddha highlighted situations that he called *dukkha* which are times when there is danger of spiritual loss. At such time he cautioned us to exercise especial vigilance. If we act wisely at the spiritual level there will be an increase of love in the world – a spiritual gain for all. This is what religion is trying to ensure.

We could say that this is about morals and religion is certainly concerned with morals, but morality is not really the most fundamental aspect of what we are talking about. Spirit is more about morale. When there is much love, people will be in good morale. When there is much corruption, morale will be low. Low morale means low spirits. We all intuitively recognise the importance of the spirit. An act can be moral in a formal sense yet still not be performed in a good spirit. Spirit is the life of love. Morality is the formalisation of that spirit into rules and fixed forms. Ethics is one stage even further and eventually we arrive are mere regulations. This sequence from spirit to morals to ethics to regulations is a progress from the metaphysical toward the merely physical and behavioural.

A completely secular society pruned of metaphysics as far as is possible would have many regulations, but there would be little heart in them. Following them would be conformity, but it would not, of itself, bring love into the world. Do you recognise this situation? Do you see it at work in our culture?

So, to stay with the main point, spirituality involves a calculus that is different from the purely materialistic. In our modern world we are very concerned with calculation. We attribute monetary values to things so that we can make calculations about them. We are also concerned with popularity and votes, but even though you are popular, it does not necessarily mean that you are really loved. Materialism is concerned with quantity, religion with quality.

What is the difference between the spiritual calculus and the materialist calculus? The difference is that the latter is a zero-sum game. If one gains another loses. The total remains constant. Items can be rearranged, but there are only so many. This is scientific and logical. In physics there is no new creation, only transformation. If there were three before, there will be three afterwards. The items may be rearranged, but you cannot get seven out of three. However, at the spiritual level it is quite different. Both can gain at the same time. Love can appear out of nowhere. In Buddhism this is called "flowers appearing in the sky". The sky means emptiness. The Indian word is shunyata. Shunyata is a very important word in Buddhism. It is, however, much misunderstood. You can read many abstruse theses about shunyata and at the end of reading them you have the impression of having listened to something very clever, but still have no idea what it was.

Here, however, it is clear that shunyata means that something can come out of nothing: flowers appear in the sky. We shall have more to say about sky flowers in a later section.

Flowers, in this expression, means results or consequences. Flowers are the consequence of seeds growing. It is sometimes said that Buddhism is about cause and effect and this kind of statement makes it sound very scientific; but Buddhism is really about flowers appearing in the sky: consequences appearing out of nothing. How does something come out of nothing? You may remember that in the play by Shakespeare, King Lear says "Nothing comes of nothing." He says this because he does not recognise the love that his youngest daughter Cordelia has for him. It is on this failure to recognise her true love that the tragedy of the play hinges. Because the love is not recognised, Lear goes mad, Cordelia meets an untimely death, and the selfish characters dominate events. This is a parable for our world.

Something comes out of nothing when there is love. Love is something kind done for nothing. If it is done for something it is not really love. Love is, by nature, completely gratuitous. Love is always something out of nothing and when love is received it multiplies. Flowers appear in space. They fall all around us. We gather them in baskets and offer them to Buddhas. Such flowers appear and disappear, but we need not be distressed at their disappearance as there will always be more appearing out of the sky. The whole nature of Buddhist spirituality is flowers appearing in the sky.

To see such flowers one needs to have hazy eyes. Hazy eyes are the eyes of love. You know that when a person is in love you see a hazy shine in their eyes. Such a person is walking on air. Everything that happens is a cascade of flowers out of space. When a person has such hazy eyes, all other people become flower vendors.

Once the Buddha held up a flower and winked. Only his disciple Kashyapa understood. Because of this the Buddha invited Kashyapa to share his seat. After the Buddha died, Ananda wanted to know what Kashyapa had got from the Buddha. "What did Shakyamuni transfer to you?" he asked. At this stage, Ananda still had the mind that believed that something must have passed from one to the other. Ananda did not understand that Shakyamuni and Kashyapa both received an abundance of flowers at the same time. Ananda had received many flowers from Shakyamuni, but he was still in the mind of spiritual materialism. He was thinking that Shakyamuni had a great store of wisdom and that he distributed it discourse by discourse. Ananda did not realise that with every discourse it was Shakyamuni who received most, for it was Shakyamuni who had the most hazy eyes.

When a person is cured of hazy eyes, they no longer see flowers in the sky. This is the state of disenchantment that is sought by worldly rationalism. That, however, is not Buddhism. Buddhism is all flowers in the sky and the sky of Buddhism is constantly appearing and reappearing, now here, now there. There are those who approach Buddhism with a mind to gain enlightenment who really want to know how to bring the sky under control so that the production and distribution of flowers can be organised in an efficient manner, or stopped altogether. Such power hungry folk, however, never notice old Shakyamuni winking.

The Absolute

The sky in which flowers appear has no east or west. We have seen how we can think of spiritual matters in terms of a different kind of calculus. The calculus of the heart defies the calculus of materialism. Where the latter knows that three minus two is one, the heart knows that giving two from three leaves at least five. These extra flowers appear in the in-between. Between one heart and another there is such a fertile empty space.

Spiritual considerations still involve a calculus. It is a very precious one, but it is still a calculus. At the absolute level there is no calculus. The space itself cannot be measured. The shunyata out of which results appear has no measurements. It is completely beyond all material notions, even though it is the matrix out of which Buddhas emerge. There is no gain in adding anything to infinity. There is no loss in taking anything away from infinity. One Buddha is a hundred Buddhas and all the myriad Buddhas appear in a single good heart. Goodness cannot be made more good or less good. The unconditioned is always unconditioned, whatever conditions may be added or subtracted. Pure love is pure love whatever the circumstances.

We do not encounter such absolute love empirically, but we judge what love we do receive by reference to it. All that happens at the spiritual level is, in some way, a reflection of the absolute. The absolute is like sunshine. If you stand in the sun you have a shadow. The shadow may be long or short. You could measure it, but what use would such a measurement be? You have the shadow because of the sunlight. The light is not measurable. It is everywhere. The sun is no less for you having a shadow. Actually, the shadow is your happiness. It follows you wherever you go, accords to your movements, demands nothing of you, merely that you stay in the light. You cannot make such a shadow by your own effort. You cannot earn or own it, but when you stand in the light it is always there, whether you pay attention to it or not.

Although the love that we encounter in the phenomenal world is never completely unconditional, it reflects the unconditional. We see the unconditional in it. It is because it reminds us of the unconditioned that it inspires us, sometimes moving us to tears. These tears are tears of faith: they come when our habitual defences fall away. We do not just receive the quantity of love that is proportional to the one act or the one gift, we receive a faith in infinite love that transcends this moment, this instance, this quantum of activity.

An unconditional lover would always be there for one, but even the best mother cannot always be there for her child. Nonetheless, the child senses in the mother's love that more complete love that it is a token of. This is what gives the child trust. The child does not trust the mother only in proportion to the amount that the mother has done for the child.

The moon of ultimate love is reflected in the dewdrop of the mother's tears. What happens at the spiritual level is spiritual inasmuch as it relates to the absolute beyond. Thus, in a spiritual life, one is, as it were, always going beyond. Every spiritual act is an instance of something that has gone beyond the merely material. This is the Buddhist life, to have *gone, gone, gone beyond, gone completely beyond* again and again (Prajna Paramita

Hridaya Sutra). Such is awakening. Such is the highest fulfilment.

A Buddha, therefore, is in the physical world, but always going beyond it; going beyond it in fact, but not by contrivance. The going beyond is not a deliberate activity or a practice; going beyond is just the natural effect of *living in the sky*. This is the exact opposite of a reductionist way of thinking. It is an expansionist way, a great way, endlessly opening further. It is a life that is mindful of nirvana. It is faith. The person of faith walks on air and lives in the sky. Were they to start to calculate gain or loss they would immediately fall to earth. It is people who are foolish in this way who are enlightened. On them, the sun is always shining. Such is Buddhism.

5: Religion as a Social Phenomenon

Religion as the Key to Changing Society

In 1956 Dr. Bimrao Ambedkar converted to Buddhism. Who was he and why did he do this? Ambedkar was a politician. He had become the leader of the "untouchables", the impoverished hundreds of millions in India. The untouchables were excluded from the caste system and treated as a lower form of life, to be abused and exploited at will by the caste Hindus. Caste was an essential part of Hindu religion.

Ambedkar had been part of India's struggle for independence from Britain. In this, he was an associate of Gandhi. When independence came, Ambedkar wrote the constitution of the new India. There are more statues to Ambedkar in India than to any other individual. However, Ambedkar and Gandhi parted company. This was over the issue of caste. Gandhi wanted to reform the caste system. Ambedkar wanted to abolish it. Gandhi was a Hindu and he saw Hinduism as part of the essential identity of India. Ambedkar realised that he could not achieve his goal by political means alone. A deeper change was required. A merely rational approach would not succeed. He therefore decided that he had to choose a new religion. Only by a change at the most fundamental level could caste really be abolished.

Ambedkar examined the several possibilities which included becoming a Christian, a Moslem or a Sikh. In the end he chose Buddhism. Not all religions are the same. Each has a view of human nature and an associated sense of the ideal ordering of society. Religion is not just an individual matter. This is one of the reasons that modernism is uneasy with religion. The modernist project is closely associated with the idea of a secular state. Historically the balance between church and state has often been a key factor in the dynamic of societies. The Pharaoh of Egypt was king, but perhaps even more importantly, he was also chief priest. The Protestant monarchs of England achieved a similar status. However, in the Catholic world, including England before the Reformation, the church was often the only power in the land with the authority to defy the monarch and it was the balance between the secular and spiritual powers that gave society its dynamism. In modern times, the state appears to have triumphed in this struggle and reduced religion to being a matter of individual choice. You do not have a choice about which government you want to live under, but you can choose your religion in much the same way as you choose your house or car. This gives us the sense that religion is not particularly important. In a certain way, the state has once again become the religion. However, this unification of powers is dangerous leaving the individual at the mercy of a sovereign power that has no limits.

However, Ambedkar realised that even in a supposedly democratic society there is always a substratum of attitudes that are deeply set in the religious consciousness of that culture. Even those who publicly and consciously reject the traditional religion are often still thoroughly impregnated with its attitudes and values. We see this in our own case. Many of the debates within contemporary Buddhist studies in the West are not really about Buddhist issues. They use Buddhism and Buddhist language as a medium, but the substance of the debate has far more to do with age old preoccupations of Western society – justice, judgement, consciousness, dualism, morality, ends and means, democracy, individualism, guilt and forgiveness, and many others – most of which derive from the monotheistic religions that have dominated these regions historically. Many of these concepts have now been imported into Buddhism, without having real roots in Buddhist tradition. The Buddhist texts have almost nothing to say about judgement, guilt and forgiveness, for instance. They have much to say about compassion, kindness and renunciation, but these are different concepts implying a different world view. Although Buddhism has plenty written about morality, Buddhists in Buddhist countries are far less concerned about moral issues than people brought up in Christian ones. Buddhism, consequently, has a reputation for tolerance.

If Buddhism is to have a real impact in the West it will not be by being itself subsumed into existing Western discourse. At the moment we are still in the stage of asking what Buddhism has to say about our age old obsessions. However, what Buddhism really proposes is something much more difficult and ambitious, namely a transformation of the religious sensibility of Western people, including those who do not think of themselves as religious. The often hidden religious assumptions that a culture harbours lie at its deepest level. Acknowledging that Buddhism is a religion means acknowledging its challenge to these most fundamental layers of our world view.

The current campaign of many intellectuals to reform Buddhism as no longer a religion is an attempt to avoid, or blunt, this challenge. If Buddhism can be restructured in its fundament so as to conform to the secular, atheistic, rational, sceptical modern or postmodern paradigm, then the real challenge that Buddhism presents to our ways of thinking, feeling, acting and being can be averted. Such a campaign, however, is surely a forlorn hope. Buddhism has greater depth. One is reminded of the early attempts of Jesuit missionaries to convert Japan to Catholicism. They came to think of Buddhism as the most devilish of religions. This was because their early efforts seemed to meet with remarkable success, yet, in the end, were found to be empty. Buddhists were happy to be converted and to participate in what the Jesuits had to offer, because they were inclusive. Participating in Catholicism did not, to them, mean giving up Buddhism. Buddha had a big enough heart to encompass the newcomers and make them feel welcome. The Westerners were locked in attitudes of exclusivity. Adherence to one religion meant violent rejection of all others. That is not the Buddhist approach. Similarly, Buddhism coming West will accommodate Western prejudices. The Dalai Lama will happily say that if science proves something that is incompatible with Buddhist doctrine Buddhism will change, knowing that science never actually proves anything of a religious nature since that is not its province. Buddhism is willing to put on scientific looking clothes if that will enable some Western educated people to participate and take an interest long enough to catch at least a little bit of the spirit of the Dharma, but to think that this means that Buddhism has really changed in its essence would be a mistake. The treasure of Buddhism is the loving, all-embracing heart of Buddha and the blessing of his Dharma, his fundamental understanding of human nature, and that nature is essentially religious. Eventually, it is the religious nature of Buddhism that will convert the West, or there will never be a real Buddhism in the West.

Some of the most effective apologists for Buddhism in the contemporary world (using the term apologist in its positive sense) suggest that it is impractical or even undesirable for Western people to change their religion. Both the Dalai Lama and Thich Nhat Hanh have made comments along these lines. I agree with them that a real change of religion is rare and difficult, but I suggest that it may well be what is needed, nonetheless. Ambedkar thought that such a change could be the salvation of India, freeing it from its seeming addiction to the oppression and divisions of castism. No more shallow change would do the trick. Legislation merely scratches the surface.

By taking this stand, Ambedkar has become a bodhisattva saint, revered by the poor. The slogan "Jai Bhim!" meaning "Long live Dr. Bhimrao Ambedkar" has become a kind of religious mantra for millions which has built a connection between the formerly powerless in a way that has already substantially changed their position in society such that one of their number has now been president of the largest state in India, a region more populous than most European countries. Intellectuals may deride simple faith, but it is precisely this kind that moves the depths of a society in the sustained way that merely intellectual ideas rarely do. Religion builds civilization and even our supposedly secular societies are built on a foundation of confidence in principles left over from religion. It must be highly doubtful whether a truly rational society could long endure, or even be constructed in the first place. Much science fiction has been written around the theme of the almost inevitable cruelty of any such social arrangement. The brief periods in history when it has been approached, as under the legalists in ancient China, have not been great successes. A truly civil society requires ingrained civility in its populous and this, in turn, needs faith. It cannot be merely legislated.

His devotees believe that Dr. Ambedkar was moved by the same spirit of compassion as Shakyamuni Buddha and they accord him the same transcendent status. On the strength of this faith rests a whole way of being with one another that has not been imposed by rule but is a function of goodwill emanating from faith. No wholesome society can do without some such. This does not mean that one particular faith is correct and all others wrong; it means that faith itself is an essential element in social cohesion and those who deride it are deceiving themselves for they too are coasting on the momentum of old faith so long established that it has become second nature. Their efforts to demolish it, however, will not stand their grand-children in good stead. The latter will have to live in a more heartless world where the predominant image is the soulless machine rather than a heaven of loving beings. For the sake of humane society it is more important to implant faith than to demolish it. What has gone wrong in our corner of the world is that while the power of faith is needed to create social good, any power once created can also be used for evil and at times in history religion has turned sour in this way to a degree that has left many disenchanted and repelled. However, what is needed is faith that is benign, not a faithless desert.

Ordinary Faith in Practice

What is religion for an ordinary devotee? If you go to a Buddhist country, what does Buddhist practice look like? You will see Buddhist devotees go to the temple. They probably make some prostrations to the Buddha or one or more of the other holy figures, represented by statues. They may well make an offering of food, candles or incense. Then they sit and make prayers or simply spend some time in the holy precincts absorbing the atmosphere. These days there is an infinitely graduated spectrum between the devout devotee and the mere tourist, but all absorb something from the calm of the ambiance and the associations of meaning of the symbolism with which the situation is replete. It is unlikely that either tourist or devotee will do any formal meditation – that tends to be reserved to a small minority of specialist sacerdotal practitioners. Rather they might spend some time with the monk or priest talking about personal or family matters, or about events at the temple, or sharing news, or they might be involved in some temple based social activity. Many temples are involved in social service of one kind or another. The whole tenor of the visit is devotional, personal, and generally relaxed. They go away spiritually refreshed, feeling closer to the Buddha, supported by his transcendental power.

The above description could be in Sri Lanka, Nepal, Vietnam or Japan. The actual artwork on the walls might be different, the robes of the monks might be different colours, the liturgy might be different, the beliefs might not be identical, but beliefs, liturgy, iconography, vestments, and a general ambiance of sanctity and profundity there would be; Buddhism, after all, is a religion, and it is to be enjoyed as such.

The West has acquired some unfortunate attitudes in relation to religion which do not serve us well. Many of these are related to our individualistic, competitive culture, itself a product of older ideas of individual salvation and a sense of the necessity of self-justification, all vestiges of religious attitudes that underpin our Western world view. Some while ago I was paying my respects at a Shinto temple in Japan. Shinto is the national indigenous religion of Japan, distinct from Buddhism which arrived in those islands via Korea and China. You might ask, what is a Buddhist doing paying respects in a Shinto temple, but, in Japan, this is perfectly normal. I noticed a group of people similarly dressed, presumably in the convention of some enterprise or other, and I asked my translator who they were. She told me that they were the staff of a nearby factory who had come to have their work for the coming year blessed by the Shinto priest. Betraying my Western education and prejudice, I asked if that meant that everybody in that enterprise were of the Shinto persuasion. "Oh, no," she replied, "They will probably go to the Buddhist temple next week."

This inclusive attitude that sees all religion as beneficial, all faith as basically helpful, is surely sane. Furthermore, it enables everybody to participate in everything if they so desire. Here the element of competition between faiths, and, indeed, between temples of the same faith, is not absent, but it has not risen to the destructive crescendo that we have too often been witness to in our own history. It remains at a level where it is stimulating without being pernicious. Surely this is the ideal. The common idea that it must be the case that only one religion or ideology can have merit and all others must be the work of the devil is a kind of social insanity. Somehow we need to instil a new ethos in regard to religion as a whole. This does not mean going to the other extreme of asserting that all religions are the same and there is nothing to choose between them. They are not and there is. It is important that people think about what they do truly have faith in and to think that all faith is identical is as wide of the mark as thinking that all faith is error. The fact is that in a world of such uncertainty as the one we inhabit one cannot but live by faith in many respects and it matters what one has faith in. It matters, but that does not mean that one needs to fight with those who think differently. True faith should give one the strength to be open minded and big hearted. Narrow-mindedness is really a symptom of fear rather than faith, a sign that one dreads the possibility of one's faith being challenged. Such dread is really a sign of underlying doubt.

The person of simple faith bowing to the Buddha in the temple is not concerned that tourists are taking photos and students are sitting in the courtyard discussing the film they saw on television last night. All of life is here and the Buddha smiles on all, blessing each in their own way. Buddhism is religion, but it is not puritan.

The term economics comes from the Greek word for a household. Economics is about how you run your household. Thus it is a metaphor. Economic policy is about how to manage the budget of a country as if it were a household. Now Buddhism, famously, is a religion that only accords the householder life a partial share in the community. Buddhism has always been, in effect, a co-operation between those who are householders and those who have renounced the householder life. Buddhist economics, we could then say, embraces the possibility of its own negation.

Our Western approach to economy advances a range of values. These include growth, maximisation of profit, efficiency, saving, capital accumulation, investment, deferred gratification, self-sufficiency and competition. Buddhism does not so much negate these values as point out that they are not the whole picture. They are only half of a yin-yang wholeness that must somehow also accommodate their real opposites, namely letting go, generosity, quality of life, sharing, unburdenment, faith, gratitude, self-forgetting and co-operation. It is not so much that these are alternatives; more that they together all contribute to the wholeness of life. Furthermore, in a healthy society there will be some people who embody some of these values and other people who embody others and all will have an honourable place in the whole. The Buddha taught that a healthy society is one that honours those who live the renunciant life. He also taught that a good governor ensures that those who have the will and ability to engage in wholesome industry have the means to do so. It is a question of wholeness and mutual appreciation.

Further, it is a question of ends. Buddha teaches us how to avoid being defeated by spiritual danger. Buddhism is not opposed to people generating wealth, but it asks the question what such wealth is for. From this perspective, wealth that is used merely to feather one's own nest and generate power and privilege is an empty achievement. It only puts one in a position of greater spiritual danger. The more power you have the more good or harm you can do. Whether you have much or little the spiritual questions remain much the same. Do you appreciate what you have and do you use it for the greater good?

And it is a question of means. If the accumulation of wealth becomes an end in itself then it is likely to ride roughly over others. Thus we arrive at the question, can we build wholesome communities by wholesome means; can we do so with kindly hearts?

Western economics is thought of as being a science independent of religion. However, the values it encompasses reflect a particular worldview with its roots in Christianity. The idea of each person pursuing their own good derives from the idea that each soul must justify itself and achieve its own salvation. However, it is not by satisfying the ego's belief in our own superhuman nature and limitless self-entitlement that we find salvation. That way lies only frustration and a burdensome life of one crisis after another. Only when we see our poverty can we find the treasure, for the treasure does not lie inside oneself. Investigating the reality of our own case and finding a spiritual treasure beyond self work together. We cannot find the treasure without finding our poverty first, but we cannot face our poverty without having a treasure to rely upon. This is the impossible situation of samsara where the conceit of self allows no chink of light to enter. There is no way out of this prison by logic, or effort, or self-perfection. Only faith can open the door, faith that yields wisdom, faith that allows a sideways leap out of the trap of the ego chasing its own tail. Buddhism is a religion that opens the door. Buddha is a power that is not oneself. We can note in passing that Christianity originally and fundamentally also offers a similar option and it is a shame that the individualistic aspect has become so over-emphasised as secularism has taken hold.

The Western mind would like to reframe Buddhism too in the individualist mode, reducing the power of Buddha by emphasising his merely human status and playing up whatever reference to self-power can be found in the Buddhist sources. Such reference is not lacking, but it is only one part of what Buddhism amounts to and not even the most important part. For most Asian Buddhists, Buddhism is a reassurance not a goad.

Art & Architecture

Because Buddhism has a wealth of writing on the mind, some may say that it is basically a psychology. They might, however, just as well say that it is a school of art and architecture. The manner in which many people have their first encounter with Buddhism is through the imagery and structures that it gives rise to and these structures and images are some of the most potent Buddhist missionaries. A goodly portion the garden centres in the Western world now stock Buddha images and even in some of the most secular and rational centres

of modernity, like Amsterdam, one will see seated Buddhas smiling benignly all over town.

Some of the finest architecture in Asia is Buddhist. Huge structures have been created, rivalling those of ancient Egypt. It is religion that generates this kind of manifestation. Building the acropolis or the great pyramid was a function of collective religious devotion. No less is this the case with the Shwedagon Pagoda, the Potala Palace, the Kamakura Buddha and the innumerable other structures that Buddhists have created to celebrate and transmit their faith.

These structures have effect. These effects are both memorial and prospective. Buddhist temples and monuments often commemorate persons and events from the past and this activity is energetically active to this present day as anybody who visits Bodh Gaya in India can immediately see for him or herself. The marking of holy sites commenced immediately after the death of the founder and did so on his instruction. They are and were intended to be places of worship and pilgrimage, reflection and spiritual restoration.

While Buddhism is not opposed to settled society, it has always also valued the roaming life and pilgrimage has thus been a natural part of Buddhist practice. Pilgrims travel, which means that they leave their regular life with all its established conditioning and place themselves in a less hemmed-in situation. This is itself a kind of liberation. They do so in the service of a holy purpose. Thus, if one is spending a month, or several months, travelling to a holy site one is going to be thinking about and reflecting on holy themes for that time and one is going to be absorbing the meaning not merely at a mental level but with every step along the way, and even more potently if, as is the case with some Buddhist pilgrims, some or all of the journey is made doing prostrations with one's whole body. This is the real meaning of mindfulness: to undertake some activity that fills one's mind, heart, body and soul with holy meaning.

The manner in which Buddhist sites are constructed is no less full of holy meaning. A Buddhist temple is an attempt to represent a small sample or token of heaven on earth. A Buddhist expects to be reborn and hopes to be reborn somewhere beneficent. Such a place is a place where a Buddha exists and where the influence of that Buddha prevails. Such a place is called a Pure Land, Pure Abode or Buddha Field. These are the heavens of Buddhism and Buddhists attempt to create, as near as can be, places in this world where one will catch a little of the flavour of such a land. Thus the buildings, architecture, imagery, gardens and total ambiance all contribute to giving such a suitable effect, helping the devotee to become accustomed to living in heaven as his or her true home, so that when the time comes, they will naturally gravitate there. The style may vary hugely: a colourful Tibetan monastery differs aesthetically in a radical way from a Zen garden, but spiritually they have the same soul.

It should be readily apparent that the religious purpose can find expression in many styles and that it gives rise to great skill and creativity. I have delighted in watching craftsmen in Vietnam adding dragons to pillars on new or reconstructed temples. I have been amazed to see huge Buddha images in Korea that look as if they weigh a hundred tons and then being told that they are actually made of paper and can be carried by a couple of monks cooperating and that this art was developed because in history this coast was vulnerable to Japanese pirates and the monastics needed to be able to remove their images at short notice on occasion. Religion generates such richness through its mix of practicality and holy purpose. These structures have a purpose, which is the cultivation of serenity and faith. However they are not utilitarian nor are they constructed in order to boost an artist to celebrity status. Making such things is itself a prayer, and, often, a collective one.

A pagoda is not a very practical structure if one's idea of life is utilitarian. Most of it is symbolic decoration. The pagoda developed out of the stupa. A stupa is a burial mound. Originally mounds were thrown up over the ashes and relics of saints, ideally those of the Buddha himself. These mounds are not unlike the stone age mounds to be seen around Stonehenge in England or many other parts of Europe. This, therefore, is probably an age old human practice. Gradually the mounds evolved in style. Balustrades were added, then crowning structures that symbolised the sage and the teaching. Gradually the crowning structures grew higher, and ultimately we have the pagoda of East Asia.

Relics have thus been a central element in traditional Buddhist religion from the very beginning. This is something that modernity finds difficult to understand. What is the use of old bones?

Buddhism is about the sacred inter-penetrating the mundane. A classic definition of religion is that religion exists wherever there is a distinction between the mundane and the sacred. Once such a distinction is made then there is the issue of the relationship between the two.

Religious practice is concerned with this relationship. How does the mundane relate to the sacred and how does the sacred enter into the mundane? How are ordinary beings like ourselves to relate to the unconditioned?

Buddhas are people who have awoken to the unconditioned. The unconditioned permeates their lives and they partake of it. Hence they are, as our friend Dogen says, "eternal Buddhas", even though they are, simultaneously, occupants of mundane bodies. Relics are evidence that such beings have walked this earth and, for the devotee, they are a link, a connection, with the body-mind of those remarkable beings.

This is not an idea that is totally alien to our own culture. In the Middle Ages in Europe, pilgrimage to places where the relics of saints were enshrined was regarded as one of, if not the most, meritorious practices. Receiving the blessing of dead saints was felt to be as or more powerful than the mass. People need intermediaries between themselves and the ultimate. This is how religion works and is how life is sanctified. Much of this precious tradition has been lost or vandalised in our culture's rush toward material accumulation. We own more, but mean less.

Even in the Buddha's lifetime there were relics. When he cut his hair people kept it and revered it. This is a bit like keeping a lock of the hair of one's beloved. You can put it in a locket and hang it on a chain around your neck or keep it in a special place. Touching or looking at it engenders strong feelings of love and devotion.

Thus, Buddhist art and architecture emerge as part of a religiosity that embraces pilgrimage, relics, blessings, heavens, holiness and sanctity. Without this religious root we would not have such fruits, nor would they have any meaning.

At Ajanta in India there are cave temples. It is a remarkable site. The temples are carved out of the cliff face. An overlying strata of hard rock is used as the ceiling. The temples were made by cutting into the face just below this strata and then cutting downwards, hollowing out chambers and leaving rock where one wanted walls and so on. Even the Buddha images are simply the living rock sculpted away, not imported figures carved elsewhere. Such industry is prodigious and ingenious. What was it for?

It appears that there were two periods of major activity at Ajanta, a few hundred years apart. In each case numerous temples were constructed and each would have housed a small community. A person could have come and spent some time in one before moving on to another. Probably each would have had some degree of specialisation in one or another aspect of Buddhist practice or doctrine. Thus one could acquire a comprehensive Buddhist training and education by spending some years in such a complex of holy dwellings.

One thing that is immediately noticeable is the difference of style between the older caves and the later ones. The latter each have a Buddha image and sitting places suitable for meditation, prayer, or for listening to lectures. The former, however, have very little in the way of seating, but have a large central stupa with a walkway going around it. It is evident that these earlier temples were meant for a devotional practice that involved circumambulating the relics contained in the stupa. For ordinary Buddhists, this religion was originally centrally focussed on such worship and the transmission of spiritual power and healing that it brought.

Archeology at other sites also suggests that in the earliest life of what we might call the primitive Buddhist community there were two main styles of activity. There were dwellings set apart for meditation for a small number of renunciants, but the main, larger structures were clearly intended for devotional activity centred on stupas.

In some ways it is rather odd that modern Western people, who are not renunciant by nature or inclination, have seized upon the activity of renunciants as the one part of Buddhism that appeals to them and have somehow turned it into a technique, not for leaving the world, but rather for more effective participation and survival in it. A kind of reversal has taken place here. The world-renouncing part of Buddhism has been grasped and turned into its opposite, while the world-affirming part has been ignored and rejected.

Of course, this is an oversimplification, even if it does throw some light on some aspects of the matter in hand. Buddhism has never been reduced to merely two types of activity or two styles of organisation. There have been hermits, monasteries, wandering mendicants, priests with temples, lay community leaders, charitable enterprises, populist movements, involvement in politics and high society as well as community development and poverty relief, and a multitude of cultural, educational, scientific and social ventures. Out of this has come a wide variety of buildings, monuments, statuary, and settlements.

It is characteristic that Buddhism has generated communities. Sometimes these have been monastic or have had a monastic element, but generally we are talking about complex social organisation in which religious professionals, using the term professional in its old fashioned sense to mean those whose full time occupation was a profession of faith, interacted with lay devotees. The isolated monastery was the exception rather than the rule. Even in China where monasticism reached an advanced development, a large monastery might have several thousand inhabitants, a few hundred at most of whom were "meditation monks". Such a community might have its own fields, storehouses, shops, services and factories, the whole organised around an image of enacting here in the mundane world something of the spirit of a true Buddha Field.

6: A Popular Misconception

The Mindfulness Phenomenon

Recently there has been a great deal of attention in the West to something called mindfulness. There are now thousands of books and articles on this subject and a very large number of practitioners of the art. Mindfulness as currently understood in the West is a way of paying attention to and seeing clearly whatever is happening as it is happening. It is suggested that it now provides us with a scientifically researched approach to cultivating clarity, insight, and relief from anxiety, depression, and a variety of other common psychological ills. It is a form of deliberate non-judgemental attention, in the present moment, that has benefits in terms of enhanced personal effectiveness and having an easier life.

Now we all know that mindfulness derives from Buddhism. It is the first of what are called the Seven Factors of Awakening. So is this what people think that Buddhism is about? If so, then they are surely misinformed. I wish here to suggest that this contemporary popular "mindfulness" is different from the mindfulness that was taught by Buddha as one of the factors of spiritual awakening and to look at what this transformation tells us about the manner in which Buddhism is being modified.

In an effort to present an edited version of Buddhism, Western commentators have certain favoured texts. One of these is the Sattipatthana Sutta. The Satthipatthana is about mindfulness. We know this because it has the word "sati", which is the Pali for mindfulness, in the title. "Patthana," from *upatthana* means "having close at hand". Commonly, the title is rendered "The Setting Up of Mindfulness" which gives the whole thing an air of being a technical manual. One can immediately see how this plays into the Western preference. The title could, however, be rendered as "Having Mindfulness Always at Hand."

The early part of this text includes many references to awareness and attention, such as "When reaching out his arm he is aware that he is reaching out his arm," "when taking a long breath he is aware that this is a long breath," and so on. This has led many readers to believe that mindfulness is awareness and that these statements are exercises for developing it. If this were correct, then the import of the text would be that there is a skill to be developed and this is how you do it. The skill in question would be some kind of attention, or awareness, or enhanced consciousness. Undoubtedly many people now think that developing such a skill and maintaining it for the longest possible periods is what Buddhism is all about. This idea is now so widespread that it is becoming true. However, this is a mistaken idea of what was meant by mindfulness in the teachings of Shakyamuni Buddha.

A more careful reading reveals that the beginning of the text includes the passage:

"A bhikkhu goes to the forest, or to the foot of a tree, or to an empty hut and sits down; he folds his legs, sits up straight and establishes mindfulness in front of him. With mindfulness established thus, he breathes in, with mindfulness thus he breathes out…" It is clear from this that the text is not about how to set up mindfulness, for it starts with mindfulness already established. What the text is saying is that, in the context of mindfulness already at hand, the bhikkhu practises awareness. Mindfulness and awareness are not the same thing. The first point is that one's mindfulness be close at hand. With this established, one uses awareness to examine various aspects of mind and body. The aim is not to cultivate awareness but to use it. What for?

Awareness is a kind of vigilance. The first awareness that is practised is of bodily functions. Why do we need to be wary of bodily functions? Because it is tempting to see the body as oneself. However, if one keeps one's mindfulness, which is to say, one's faith, close at hand while observing the body one will be able to see the "fundamental nature of what is arising" (*samudayadhamma*), and one will then not be taken in by it. Rather, one will see that the body is just a body. It arises and it passes away. It is not oneself.

What is the spiritual significance of this? Mindfulness is not awareness, mindfulness is "keeping in mind". It is a form of memory. What does a bhikkhu (or any Buddhist) keep in mind? He keeps in mind the Buddha and the Dharma, which are a true and permanent refuge. They are true and permanent because they are metaphysical and so not subject to decay in the way that physical things are. What is the purpose of keeping this true refuge in mind while contemplating the body? It is to realise that the body is not a true refuge.

The text goes on in similar way to show that feelings are not a true refuge and mind is not a true refuge. The bhikkhu realises that they are not true refuges by observing that they arise and fall away. Similar practice and logic is found in many other Buddhist texts. For somebody who has no refuge beyond what is physical, the direct perception of impermanence could be too terrifying to contemplate, so it is only possible to do this fully if one has another refuge that is beyond the physical already established. The true refuge does not pass away. Thus mindfulness empowers awareness and awareness thus consolidates mindfulness. Mindfulness, here, refers to correct faith: i.e. to what is worth keeping in mind. Right faith is consolidated by paying attention to the unsatisfactory nature of wrong faith. People who do not keep the Buddha and the Dharma in mind, fail to do so because they rely upon their own bodies, feelings and minds instead. They have faith in things that are impermanent, unreliable and prone to provoke affliction.

Mindfulness is not attention and it is not a skill. It is keeping the Dharma in mind and not being taken in by the notion that body, mind and feelings constitute a refuge. Here I mean, of course, mindfulness in Buddhism as in the text. In modern mindfulness practice, mindfulness has come to mean awareness, or even full consciousness, and it is definitely a skill. This is, however, not even the original meaning of the term mindfulness in English. When my mother told me to be mindful of my manners, she was not saying anything about awareness, or living in the present moment; in fact, she was warning me against being too much in the present moment. “Be mindful of your manners,” meant remember them. Don't be so carried away by things of the present moment that you forget more important things. My mother's usage of the term was much closer to that of Buddha than what has become of it in the present vogue for enhanced present state attention.

Enhanced present state attention is clearly something that fits well with the value system of a hedonistic culture where immediate self-gratification is held as an ideal, but this is not Buddhism.

Attentiveness is not a goal in itself. Being aware 24/7 would not constitute any kind of salvation, in fact, it would be exhausting. Attentiveness is a phenomenon that arises in the course of learning something, or acting in circumstances when things are uncertain. In a healthy person it arises appropriately and falls away again when not needed. Awareness is essentially about vigilance. It is related to wariness. The Buddha wants us to be wary of the things that might corrupt us and he wants us to use our attentive awareness to find out things that, once known by such experience and investigation, will continue to inform our attitude to life, both consciously and unconsciously.

Awareness, vigilance, has a place in Buddhism. Buddha wants us to learn things, including various forms of self-restraint, and in the course of such learning, we need to be attentive. Buddha wants us to investigate. He wants us to find out for ourselves that some things are impermanent and some are not. In the course of such investigation awareness is necessary. However, once the lesson is learnt, the attentiveness is no longer so necessary because the lesson has become part of oneself. It becomes something that one is mindful of at the appropriate time.

We can see this function of awareness in the learning of any skill. If you have learnt to drive a car you will know that there was a phase during which you were acutely attentive to every bodily movement. This was because your feet were not accustomed to moving the brake and clutch at the same time while your hand moved to the gear lever and your eyes to the rear view mirror. However, once you had learnt to drive you no longer had to think consciously about these things. Having changed gear thousands of times it became second nature. You could do it while your brain was engaged in a complex conversation with the person sitting next to you. The awareness that had been vital at an earlier stage was no longer needed because the lesson had been learnt. You do not learn to drive in order to live in a state of awareness, you practise some awareness in order to learn to drive. Awareness, as a state of attention, is not a goal in itself.

Finally, in the last major section of the text, the bhikkhu contemplates the fundamentals of Buddha's teaching, considering the things that are to be remembered in relation to what he can observe happening in himself. This last section which is clearly the culmination of the text, is concerned wholly with investigating the Buddha's teachings. These are not physical objects. They are not physical things observed in the here and now. They are enduring principles of life and meaning, things that it is good to be mindful of. In the course of the text, the practitioner has progressed from studying the material aspects of life and finding them unsatisfactory refuges to considering the metaphysical ones. He sees that these fundamentals are, indeed, just the fundamentals of our situation.

The overall purpose of the text, therefore, is not to establish a skill called mindfulness synonymous with awareness, but to use awareness to deepen the practitioner's understanding of and faith in the things that, as a Buddhist, he is to be mindful of. It is not about learning a skill, it is about grounding one's faith through discarding alternatives. This is not a personal effectiveness programme, though it might have some spin-off of that kind, it is about deepening faith through spiritual exercises.

At the end of his life the Buddha said:

When he dwells contemplating the body as a body, ardent, clearly comprehending, and mindful, free of desire and sorrow in regard to the world; when he dwells contemplating feelings as feelings, the mind as mind, and Dharma as Dharma, ardent, clearly comprehending, and mindful, free of desire and sorrow in regard to the world, then, truly, he is an island unto himself, a refuge unto himself, seeking no other refuge; having the Dhamma as his island, the Dhamma as his refuge, seeking no other refuge. (Mahaparinibbana Sutta)

The kind of "self-reliance" that Buddha is interested in is one in which "self" has been completely displaced by Dharma.

Buddha Mindfulness

We can also say, incidentally, that Buddhism is not about becoming more and more conscious. When something has been learnt and internalised it does not remain in consciousness all the time. Mindfulness is not continuous consciousness. The things that the mind is full of, if they are well integrated, present themselves to consciousness as and when it is appropriate for them to do so but mostly work automatically. A person who has become truly and deeply compassionate will do many compassionate things without thinking about it. They will have a generous view of other people so ingrained in themselves that it only rarely needs conscious awareness to be active. Rather than being aware of being compassionate, it is more the case that cynical or critical views of others simply do not occur in the first place. The most compassionate person is, very largely, unconsciously so. The same goes for other virtues.

What is the most important thing for a Buddhist to be mindful of? It is Buddha. Furthermore, the person of Buddhist faith is generally primarily mindful of what he or she receives from Buddha. The sense of gratitude is a key foundation of Buddhist faith. The awareness that plays a part in this is awareness of one's own failings, weakness, vulnerable nature and proneness to error. At the core of Buddhist faith is a sense of great gratitude that the Dharma has been given and continues to be given even to (or especially to) ordinary, fallible beings such as ourselves.

This attitude of humility and gratitude is a million miles removed from the attitude of the person who sees Buddhism as a series of techniques for some kind of self-perfection, enhanced self-reliance, or personal development. The Buddhist does not take refuge in self. The religious Buddhist takes refuge in Buddha and does so because of repeated awareness of the limitedness of ordinary human nature. By turning to Buddha there is the possibility of transcending such limitation by being open to receive the grace of the Dharma.

This practice of being mindful of Buddha, either by simply keeping Buddha in mind, or by some deliberate act such as calling the Buddha's name, is one of the most common practices of ordinary Buddhists in the Far East, much more widespread in the general population than doing formal meditation. This is the way that ordinary Buddhists celebrate their faith in a day to day manner and acknowledge one another. Saying *Namo Omito Fo* in China or *Namu Amida Butsu* in Japan or *Namo Adida Phat* in Vietnam constitutes a greeting, a way of wishing one another well, a personal spiritual practice, and a way of connecting any act with one's mindfulness of what is most sacred, namely the all-acceptance and saving power of the sambhogakaya-buddha Amitabha, whose name means Measureless Light.

Amitabha Buddha works in the world and in our lives when we are conscious and when we are not conscious. The aim of Buddhism is not to be in a state of hyper-consciousness all the time, but to have the right attitude so integrated that it is unconsciously present all the time. Even if caught completely off-guard, such a person will respond in a balanced, compassionate manner.

As human beings we are amply provided with unconsciousness. It is a very important part of our lives. The things that have taken real root in us are functioning in our unconscious. We need consciousness to cope with situations where something new is required, situations of learning, or of danger. Buddha would have us be conscious of the spiritual dangers in the world, the dangers to our soul, the dangers of corruption represented by greed, hate and delusion, but he would also have us so well tamed that loving, compassionate, wise and joyful responses to the situations that occur in life rise up in us spontaneously. The unconscious has its place and it is more fundamental.

Faith has a close relationship to the unconscious. Doubt is a kind of wariness. Faith, however, is a condition in which we trust. We trust that what we have taken refuge in will be working in our lives even when we are sound asleep.

The Here and Now Fallacy

In the modern definition of mindfulness one often sees references to living in the here and now or being aware in the present moment. This is often associated with increasing satisfaction in one's embodiedness. The Buddha, however, does not praise being in the present moment as something to cherish in itself and does not understand a person to be identical with their body. When the Buddha speaks of attending to what is present it is so that one can pass beyond attachment to it and arrive at spiritual liberation. In any case, it is clear that Buddha was not always paying attention to the here and now.

Earlier in this chapter I referred to the Mahaparinibbana Sutta. The idea that Buddhism is a kind of continuous alertness is confounded by the story in that text to the effect that Buddha was once so deep in meditation that he did not notice a thunderstorm that was going on around him that was so severe that two farmers were killed by it. If the Buddha could be so unaware of his immediate surroundings while still awake, one can hardly think that being acutely conscious of the here and now is the whole aim. Nor is this treated as a lapse: it is cited to show approvingly how deeply the Buddha enters into trance states in which here and now awareness is excluded.

There is a small group of utterances of Buddha that go under the name *Bhaddekaratta*. These are sometimes used as a basis for justification of the idea that Buddhism is about dwelling in the present moment. The term *bhadde-karatte*, means "to have had a good night". Various translators have wrestled with the meaning of this, but it seems a reasonable conjecture that it is the Buddha's way of advocating that others do what he did. His own spiritual awakening came in the course of a night of reflection. He is saying "I had a good night once, now you can have yours." The core of these utterances is a verse passage that gives the following message:

Don't hanker for the past, it is gone. Don't build hopes on the future, you are not there yet. Notice what your mind is up to as it is happening, and get to clarity about it. The time to make the effort is now. You can't bargain with death so this may be your only chance. Make an ardent, relentless effort and the peaceful sage will affirm that you have had your excellent night.

Now the point here is that this is not an advocacy of living in the here and now as a goal or final state. It is, rather, an advocacy of making a supreme effort at perceiving and understanding what is going on in your life by direct observation at a specific time. Once you have that understanding and conviction, the job is done. There is a clear implication that this will stand you in good stead beyond your death. Death may interfere with your work, but the work is worth doing even if you die tomorrow.

The implication is not to live for the present because tomorrow we die. It is that there is a work to do that can stand you in good stead for eternity, and the sooner you set to and do it the better.

Further on in the same passage the Buddha says that the ordinary person is defeated by what arises in the present. The nature of this defeat is that such a person regards his body, mind and feelings as himself. As they arise he identifies with them. By ordinary person, here, he says that he means one who has not been taught, become disciplined in or learned the fundamentals of the spiritual life and does not pay homage to wise teachers. Such a person lives in the present and that is his undoing.

Thus, the idea that dwelling in the here and now is a form of self-development is the exact opposite of what Buddha teaches. Buddha teaches us to notice what arises so that we can dis-identify from it and not be caught by it. We notice it so that we can realise that *this is not me, this is not mine, this is not myself* as the Buddha says in his teachings on non-self. The implication is that one's true being transcends the present moment, is not caught in feelings or thoughts, is not one's body. It is unconditional.

It is characteristic of the Buddha's religion that he tells us that we can approach the transcendental liberation through conviction arising from observation of this world. Such observation is not an affirmation of this world. It is what leads us to see the disadvantage of immersion in and attachment to this world. The Buddhist is able to live lightly in this world because he or she is not taken in by it.

Let us consider the idea of dwelling in the here and now more concretely. What would it mean to *not* dwell in the here and now? Perhaps it might mean to be asleep, yet sleep is good for the body and mind, essential even, and Buddha described himself on occasion as one who sleeps well. Perhaps it might mean to daydream, yet daydreaming is sometimes creative; what would people ever invent or create if they did not let their minds roam over wild possibilities? Perhaps it might mean reminiscence, yet reminiscence is surely part of the richness of life and even Buddha himself reminisces from time to time, especially about his one good night. The Buddha even reminisces about past lives. Perhaps it might mean thinking about things and persons not present. Yet it can hardly be a good thing to forget about one's relative in hospital simply because he is not present where one is at the time. Perhaps it might mean to speculate about imaginary circumstances, yet much of Buddha's own teaching is given by conjuring up hypothetical circumstances and analysing them.

There is a sense in which the idea of living in the here and now is trivially and inevitably the case. It is not possible to live in any other time. The here and now means the time when one is living so the statement is tautologous. When people advocate living in the here and now they do not mean simply this tautologous sense. However, if the advocacy of living in the here and now means more than this trivial sense, then it must exclude some common aspect of life and, when one reflects on the logical options, all the things that it could exclude are things that at some time or other are useful and valuable in human life.

Why then is such store set by this idea? Presumably because it represents a reductionist recipe for life. It seems to offer a pithy formula that will save one from falling into error by excluding many aspects of ordinary life. In situations of great stress, confining one's attention can be useful because it reduces the number of things to worry about. Sufficient unto the day is the evil thereof is something said by both Buddhist and Christian texts. In general, however, Buddhism is expansive and shows us how to employ all aspects of life in the service of the Dharma, not how to prune our life down to a fraction of what it was intended to be.

Evidently, there is a condition of being so attached to how things were in the past that one can give no attention or value to what needs doing now. Such a state is an obstacle to constructive living. Equally there is a condition of being in which one is so immersed in an imaginary future that one fails to do what would be necessary even to bring it about, let alone other things that need attention in the present. This too is an unfortunate state. However, it is equally true that a person who is so engrossed in the present that he makes no use of past experience and cannot plan a direction for his actions will be similarly handicapped.

More fundamentally, Buddhism is less concerned about the present moment than about eternity. Buddha's primary concern is for the long term, the very long term. In many texts the Buddha makes predictions of Buddhahood for individuals. Why would he do this if he wanted them not to think about the future? He talks of the long term effects of good and bad actions. His compassion consists in a deep concern for the long-term welfare of beings. He can see well enough that there are many actions that in the short run lead to some profit yet in the longer term lead to bad karma and the ruin of character. He does not say of such actions that one should disregard the long-term and just dwell in the here and now, forgetting the future. Rather the motive for much of the teaching that he gives is precisely to warn people of the disadvantages that lie in the future, and not just in the remainder of this life span, but in lives to come extending a vast time into the hereafter. This is a religious vision of the nature and place of persons, who are made by their intentional actions.

The modernist and postmodern paradigm has no place for other worlds and other lives and so prefers to emphasise the present since that is all that remains. The Buddha is not averse to advocating those things that are good in the present, but for him this present time is merely a tiny drop in a vast ocean of time. The Buddha's vision encompasses myriad lifetimes and endless cycles of cosmic existence. He teaches in terms that are fundamental to all times and places and that means that his teaching is one in which the dimension of time passing is an essential element. A person desists from doing something when that person sees the disadvantage of it. Advantage and disadvantage are things that unfold over time.

It is no contradiction that the Buddha says, on the one hand, *Don't hanker after the past, don't build hopes on the future, make effort today* and, on the other hand, *Think in the long term, don't be taken in by immediate appearance, don't fall into the trap of attaching to impermanent things, consider what will happen to you when, after death, on the dissolution of the body, you will reappear in some destination, either happy or in a state of deprivation* because it is the effort of today that determines that longer term future. Such emphasis as there is on the present is in order to learn something for the sake of the future.

The over-emphasis on the here and now meets the demand of people who want what Buddhism offers of peace of mind and non-violent lifestyle, yet have no belief in other lives and little concern even for their own more distant future. We live in a hedonistic, this-worldly culture. Of course, one can participate in the Buddhist community without believing the whole of what Buddhism proposes, but it is unwise to then seek to remake the whole to fit one's own preference. Very few of us actually know what happens after death. Buddhism is clearly predicated on a particular view of the matter. One should not do violence to that view just because it does not suit one to think so. You will find out the truth soon enough.

I remember that while travelling in Japan once I asked a number of people what it was about Buddhism that inspired their faith and I was repeatedly told that it was that Buddhism teaches one to have faith in such a way that one need have no fears about death, that one could, in fact, look forward to dying. It is the time of death that is the one big matter in life, I was told. Reflecting on it, I realise that there is a considerable wisdom in this attitude.

Buddhism is a sane and balanced religion. It has a religious frame which enables one to put things in an infinitely large perspective in terms of the dimension of time, the dimension of space, and the dimensions of spirit that, being metaphysical, transcend time and space. It is this infinity of perspective that enables it to be a sane and balanced middle path that does not run off to extremes. The Buddha does not insist on conformity. He simply points out what the long-terms effects are and lets us make our own decisions. Thus there is liberation within a gentle, yet uncompromising, wisdom.

7: Buddhist Belief

Faith and Conviction

Religion is associated with belief. Historically, religion in the West has often been defined in terms of belief and membership has been a matter of profession of belief. Thus a religion may have a creed in the form of a list that begins "I believe in..." To give one's assent to such a list is a formal act that makes one a member of that kind of religion.

Buddhism has never had a creed of that kind. Buddhism is a different kind of religion. The equivalent act in Buddhism is the act of taking refuge. Taking refuge does not have the same tone of assertion as assenting to a creed. In both cases one performs a personal act that gives one an identity as a member of a spiritual fraternity, but there is a difference of tone.

One could, in principle, reframe the Buddhist refuge into a formula such as "I believe in the Buddha, fully enlightened and compassionate, in his Dharma, wise and liberating, and in his Sangha, worthy and harmonious." This would still be a lot shorter and less specific than, say, the creed or the forty nine articles of the Church of England. It would be closer to a short formula such as "I believe in God the Father, God the Son and God the Holy Ghost". In these short forms one can see there is more clearly an expression of faith than there is in assent to a list of doctrinal propositions. We can see here a distinction between faith and conviction. We may say that, in Buddhism at least, faith is more important than conviction. Different Buddhists might hold different doctrinal positions and might differ considerably over the interpretation of particular texts, but this differentiation one from another in conviction is not likely to be regarded as being anything like so important as it has sometimes become in the monotheistic religions.

In Buddhism there is a strong sense that each person is on their own path, that everything they currently think is more or less deluded anyway, that such delusion may clear away one day, at a time of awakening, but that such awakening is in the future. You cannot expect people to be fully enlightened when they are just starting out. This attitude takes most of the sting out of doctrinal dispute while leaving the value of such debate intact.

Belief is sometimes a matter of choice and sometimes it is involuntary. When we are in a situation of genuinely not knowing, we might make a choice. This might be in the nature of suspending disbelief, or giving someone, or something "the benefit of the doubt". On the other hand, there are times when one simply does or does not believe something and there is nothing one can do about it. One might sometimes have some insight into where the particular belief has come from, or its origins may be hidden in forgotten history.

It is unwise, therefore, to make belief into a criterion. Beliefs change. With new evidence we find that something we used to believe no longer carries conviction for us, or, contrariwise, something that we used to have many doubts about becomes comfortable and commodious to us. Buddhism believes in such change. This does not mean that Buddhism lacks a structure of ideas about the fundamental order of things, but it does mean that if a newcomer has doubts about this or that aspect of the teaching, there is no harm in "putting it on the back burner" and coming back to it later when one has more experience.

Other Lives

It is quite clear that the Founder, Shakyamuni Buddha, believed in past lives, remembered past lives, talked about past lives and used stories of past lives as a basis of much of his teaching. He also makes numerous references to future lives. This is true in the Buddhist literature in Pali, in Sanskrit, in Chinese, and in Tibetan, in fact, universally. We cannot avoid the fact that Buddha had conviction in regard to other lives.

Not only Shakyamuni. The great historical figures celebrated by Buddhist traditions: in Zen, Bodhidharma and Dogen, in Pureland, Shan Tao, Honen and Shinran, in Tibetan Buddhism, Atisha, Milarepa, Guru Rimpoche, all the Dalai Lamas, in Theravada, Buddhaghosa, in fact, every one of the key figures in Buddhist history, based their teaching on belief in rebirth. They may have differed slightly on detail, but there is no getting away from the centrality of the importance of karma and rebirth in the foundations of all Buddhist teaching.

A modern person might or might not believe what these teachers said on the matter. That is as may be: people believe what they believe. Buddhism has not made having a particular belief on this matter a criterion of membership. Nonetheless, it would be quite improper to suggest that this is not a core belief underlying Buddhist philosophy and practice.

The central ideal of Mahayana Buddhism is the bodhisattva. The idea of a bodhisattva is a being who is on the way toward Buddhahood in a future life. A bodhisattva vows not to rest in heaven, however much such a celestial reward is due to him or her, but always to return to the worlds of sorrow in order to help other beings. This is a magnificent ideal. It is a vision that underpins selfless dedication to altruism. Now, one might say that in principle it could be possible to have such an ideal without the vision, but such a proposition does not really take full account of human nature. We humans need an encompassing vision to make sense of the smaller visions that populate our lives.

Meaning is always a multi-layered affair. Things mean what they mean in the context of some larger frame of significance. It is not possible to take something out of its frame and have it still mean the same thing. Meaning is never obtained by reduction; it is obtained by contextualisation. To know what something consists of does not tell you what it means. To know what it is part of tells you the meaning. Inevitably we cannot know the biggest, ultimate meaning, but we can intuit its general form, its vastness, it beneficence. If we exclude such great vision from our conception of life we can never have a sense of meaningfulness. Small things make sense in terms of the bigger things that they are part of. The bigger things are part of something bigger still. The biggest are inevitably out of sight and so become matters of faith. If faith is prohibited, everything becomes meaningless.

The grandeur of the Buddhist vision has, as its context, a sense of an unbounded cosmos in which persons have purpose that extends to virtually limitless periods of time. Buddhism presents a cosmic picture in which each person is part of a great purpose that will not be ended until, as the Japanese say, every tree, blade of grass, rock and mountain has entered spiritual enlightenment.

This vision is grounded in completely different principles from those of modernity and postmodernity. In these latter, the primary dogmas are, firstly, the separation of all existing things into categories of animate and inanimate, and then, within the animate the assertion that humans are highest and that everything should therefore be ordered for maximum human convenience. This is a small and small-minded vision. Thus, even contemporary concerns with ecology are almost exclusively framed within the agenda of achieving human survival, human pleasure, and human convenience. Some people have started to imagine that the non-human part of existence, which is, after all, the vast majority of it, might have some intrinsic value, but they are few. For most, the only value things can have is in terms of what they contribute to human life.

In the Buddhist vision, however, the world is not divided up in the same way. One might have been a member of another species in past lives. There might be species that we do not know of at all. There might be other planes or dimensions of existence in which exist beings that would not fit into either of our animate-inanimate categories. The Buddhist vision easily encompasses huge diversity and goes on to assert that transaction between all these diverse dimensions is a continual affair. Thus it is natural to think that although one is currently a human being, at some other time, or in some other conditions, one might be or have been something else. The human condition is regarded as a fortunate one only in the especial opportunity that it gives for hearing the Dharma and the Dharma does not imply that all other life should be subordinated to human convenience. Tibetan Buddhists thus refer to others, including other species, as "all my mothers," because, in this vision, in the infinite permutations of relationships that must be possible in virtually infinite time cycles, any other being that one encounters might at some point have been one's mother, somebody to whom one owes a supreme debt of gratitude.

Many modern people reject the idea of other lives. They might say that they are agnostic on the matter, but really this is a polite way of saying that they have conviction that there is no such thing, that we were not alive before we were born into this world in this lifetime and when we die that will be the end of the matter. Such is the supposedly rational perspective. It is one that keeps us in a narrow perception of what matters and a short term view of what is possible.

Buddha was at ease with the idea of past lives because he remembered past lives. For him it was a matter of experience. In the course of intensive meditation even a modern person may sometimes have such experience. However, so strong is the modern paradigm, that even if a modern person has such an experience they immediately begin to doubt its validity. While modernity may in principle assert the idea that each person should rely upon their own experience, it is nonetheless intolerant of any experience that does not fit into its preordained model.

The problem is that the modernist vision is much smaller than the Buddhist one. Being smaller, much of Buddhism will not fit into it.

As a modern educated person it was some time before I realised that my doubts about religion mostly did not come from my experience, but from my education. If I were really to rely solely on my own experience I would be much more of a believer and much less of a doubter. Our education teaches us to be reductionistic and to doubt or discard anything that goes outside of the secular, rationalist paradigm. Thus, at university, one is allowed to study religions or cultures as objects of interest, but one is not to take them seriously on their own terms.

In any case, it is clear that Buddhism is generally framed within an assumption that this life is not all that there is. The Buddhist belief is that what happens in this life is affected by what happened in past existences and will, in turn, affect future ones. In precise detail, different Buddhists may differ in the way that they understand these principles and in the degree of conviction with which they hold them, but the general ambiance of Buddhist thought and action is one in which there is a long term view, much longer than one lifetime. Whether one believes this is fact or fantasy, one cannot avoid the conclusion that it provides the frame that gives meaning to many Buddhist attitudes.

As a Western educated person I have sometimes found myself in the midst of this issue. In the course of an intensive meditation retreat some years ago I had a series of visionary experiences that a person from another culture, or earlier age, would have had no difficulty as identifying as memories of past lives. However, as a modern educated person my mind was divided between this obvious interpretation and a variety of more complicated rationalisations concerning how such visions could be a projection based on suppressed memories of this life interacting with personal psychological issues. This example shows how a modern person such as myself can be, as it were, caught between worlds. Actually, ideas about projection and complexes are just as metaphysical as ideas about past lives, but they are the ones that we are taught to believe in.

Although I was unable to arrive at any completely clear conviction one way or the other on this issue, there was no doubt that the experience in question had been impressive and that it could not help but be influential and formative in my spiritual life. Part of me would like to be able to have a simpler faith and another part values the ambivalent position that we thus find ourselves in, as it can be a potential source of creativity. Tensions of this kind are not always easy to live with, but they can also be the grit in the oyster that eventually yields a pearl. As people of the modern age, although we might not any longer be fully convinced by the mythology of modernity, we cannot escape from the fact that it remains a powerful element in the paradigm that underlies contemporary thought and social structures, including those we participate in every day.

Thus I find myself sometimes acting as though I have complete confidence in the idea of multiple lives and at other times as though I think this life is "all there is". Living with this ambivalence for many years has, however, led me to doubt the absolutist claims of secular rationalism. This doubt is partly post-modern, in the sense of coming to see that any absolutist claim can be relativised, and partly it is an expression of the growth of my religious faith and understanding, which recognises that while relativism may carry a certain intellectual conviction, it is an unsatisfactory basis for actually living one's life.

It can be asked if a religious way of thinking is simply wishful thinking. On the other hand, religion is concerned with those areas of meaning and commitment that intrinsically are matters of choice. It is rather as the existentialists suggest, we find ourselves thrown into this world and we have to make something of this existence. What we make of it is largely a matter of choice, which is to say of implementing our most authentic wish. I would rather commit my life to the compassion, kindness, peace, wisdom and transcendence that is Buddhism than to the relativism, self-interest, proceduralism, and coldness of a non-religious perspective. That could be called wishful thinking, but I cannot deny that that *is* my wish and that I *am* thinking it.

When I then find that those values that I laud are embedded in a different perspective on the cosmic order I feel obliged, at least, to suspend doubt until I have investigated the matter. What I find in such investigation is that the Buddhist vision of multiple lives, multiple worlds, and multiple dimensions, all interpenetrating one another, generates a sense and vision much richer than the ordinary. Whether this vision is myth or reality starts to matter less than the effect that adhering to it has on real life.

While all schools of Buddhism are founded on an assumption that there have been past and will be future lives, the actual details of this idea vary considerably from country to country. The fact is that we do not know for sure. The interpretation that I will give here, therefore, cannot be regarded as dogmatically final. It may be right, or it may not, in detail. Nonetheless, it gives, I think, a good idea of many of the important elements in the Buddhist sense of rebirth.

In the course of our life we encounter many events and circumstances and we respond to them as we do, sometimes well, sometimes badly. All the time we are learning. Some events impress themselves upon us more forcefully than others. Some are the great lessons of our life. Some things that remain in our minds are times when we were inspired. Others are times when we were defeated. Both these kinds of events can contribute substantially to our spiritual development.

Life is short and uncertain. Sooner or later death comes. At the end of our life we look back. We might have warning of our death, adjust to it gradually, and have time to reflect upon the life we have led, or, death may come suddenly and take us unawares. Buddhism regards the fact that death may come at any time as an important reflection which gives urgency to our spiritual development as well as putting the affairs of this life into a sane perspective. One will die whether one is a king or a pauper, whether one has accumulated riches or fine reputation or wasted one's life or suffered great misfortunes.

At the time of dying one reviews one's life. This may happen over a period or in a flash, but a life review takes place. Certain things stand out from one's life. They form the predominant image with which one enters the *bardo*. The bardo is the name for the between-lives state. This image will form the *bhavanga* or basal reality of one's next life.

At the time of death one enters a domain of light. One may initially feel as if one is entering a tunnel, but this tunnel emerges into light. The light is very bright. It is the light of a Buddha. Unless one is strongly dedicated to some other Buddha, it is likely to be the light of Amitabha Buddha, the Buddha of all acceptance. In any case, whichever form of Buddha has come to receive one, it is unconditional love. It welcomes one. If one enters fully into this light one will be taken immediately to the Pure Land of that Buddha.

If one is a great sage one may even see Amitabha directly. One may see the Buddha arrive accompanied by radiant *bodhisattvas* (wisdom beings). The Buddha, when he was dying, saw many celestial beings gathered. The great teacher Honen Shonin saw Amitabha come for him. Such visions are common in the case of great sages.

However, most people are not so advanced. Not only do they not see Amitabha directly, but they are unable to give themselves fully to this light. They are unable to let go and simply allow themselves to be received because they do not have sufficient faith. Thus they enter the bardo. It is thought that, in our sense of time, the bardo experience lasts up to seven weeks. For this reason Buddhists in East Asian countries may hold memorial services for the dead person every week during this period.

As one advances through the bardo one may experience a series of apparitions infused with varying colours and brightness of light. This is a dream-like experience. Some of the dreams may seem pleasant, some more like nightmares. Along the way one will feel more attracted to and involved in some of these than others. This is the manner in which one will be drawn to a new rebirth.

So one's consciousness becomes associated with a new life. Into this life one carries or is carried by the bhavanga of the previous life. This will be the primal image of one's new life. One will never become conscious of it. It will remain deep in one's unconscious, visited only in deepest sleep. Nonetheless, it will impart a flavour to one's life.

Perhaps at the end of the previous life one's predominating image was of never having got revenge on one's enemy. In this case, one will enter this new life with a predisposition toward aggression and a sense of injustice that will lead one toward vindictiveness, spite and vengeance. One does not have to act on this impulse, but it will be there. Perhaps in this new life one will fall in with good people who try to help you and give a good example and you struggle to become a good person yourself. You can do so. Because of your bhavanga, it will be a struggle. There will always be an undertow. Vindictive thoughts will rise in your mind even when you are engaged in good activities. You will have to exercise much self-restraint. At times, you will fall back into old ways.

Or, perhaps, at the end of the previous life one's predominating image was of having met a Buddha. In this new life one will have a natural attraction toward holy things. Spiritual practice will come easily to you. You will have good thoughts. Of course, you might still be corrupted. You might fall in with people who have a less healthy attitude and they might introduce you to ways of living that are unwholesome. You might become enmeshed in a way of life that yields short term rewards and pleasures, but lacks any deep satisfaction. Frequently, thoughts may arise in your mind of leaving it all and going to a monastery or seeking a teacher. You might follow these impulses, or you might not. Thus a new life will be made and, as it ends, a new review process will unfold.

Now, the first person, who has struggled all his life to be a good person against the nature that he was born with, may end this life with a new bhavanga. What may stand out for him may be the love of somebody who helped him. Thus he may go into a new life with a more clement nature. The second person, even though he was basically well inclined through this life, but wasted his opportunity, may end this life with a sense of emptiness and regret and the bhavanga with which he enters his next existence may be less fortunate. In this way beings rise and fall according to their deeds. A Buddha has the clarity to see this process unfolding whereas an ordinary person tends only to think about short term gain and personal convenience and comfort. The more spiritual a person becomes the more they are inclined to take a long term view.

This is the kind of idea that Buddhism suggests is at work in the long term unfolding of our lives. The details given here may not be precise. Buddhism is not a matter of having to believe exactly the right doctrine. The purpose of understanding a process like this is to support one's faith in the longer term, not to qualify one to pass a doctrinal exam. This theory shows how Buddhists believe that while there is continuity between lives, there is nothing unchanging that passes on through many lives. In the examples given the third lives may have little in common with the first ones.

Some General Reflections on Belief in the Afterlife

I think that what we can take from this discussion is, firstly, belief does not play as central a role in Buddhist faith as it does in, say, Christian or Islamic faith; secondly, nonetheless, the amplitude of vision of Buddhism, which is, I suggest, larger than that of modernity, tends to give rise to beliefs, some of which are at odds with reductionism, secularism or scientism; thirdly, the Buddhist view that all ordinary people (i.e. ourselves) are inevitably living in varying degrees of delusion means that there is a general expectation that wrong belief will inevitably correct itself in time as awakening progresses; which means that, fourthly, current belief is not a criterion of membership in Buddhism, yet; fifthly, beliefs have effect and thus can be a support to faith or an obstacle to it, so it would not be true to say that belief does not matter.

To summarise these conclusions differently we can say that while there are many beliefs that are characteristic of Buddhism, some of which lie outside the frame of what modernity is willing to validate, rejecting some of these is not an absolute barrier to a modern person adopting this religion yet, at the same time, these *are* Buddhist beliefs and it would be a violence to the essential spirit of the religion if all such ideas had to be excluded from it in order to give it entry to contemporary discourse. Buddhism is a religion and a very fine one and we do not need to be ashamed to believe it and to believe in it. When we do, we feel ourselves to be part of something of huge importance which does not flow from our own egos but from our faith and participation in the purpose of all the Buddhas, which is the unfolding of a great way toward universal, unconditional love, compassion, joy and peace, which is to say, to nirvana for all beings. Even if the beliefs of Buddhism eventually turned out to be wrong, there is no doubting the nobility of this vision, just as even if all the current theories of science were overturned, one should not doubt the worth of the scientific enterprise as a whole.

8: This Business About Emptiness

A Different Logic

When Buddhism talks metaphysically it often does so through the concept of emptiness. Physics is about things that are concrete. The complete absence of such is emptiness. Emptiness thus signifies what is not physical, which is to say, what is metaphysical. However, this is not itself a physical assertion: it is not saying that nothing physical exists; it is a metaphysical statement: it is saying that the logic of physics is not the logic of the Dharma.

Buddhism is a soteriological religion. It is not mere philosophy. It gives rise to philosophies, but that is not its prime purpose. Its prime purpose is salvation of beings lost in the flood of delusion. Therefore, it is not making statements about existence; it is making statements about spiritual life.

Emptiness, therefore, is not just an abstract principle by which to explain certain problems in ontology or epistemology, interesting as that might be to some scholars. Here emptiness, *shunyata* in Sanskrit, is a functional presence that makes a difference in how we live our lives.

While many people like to say that Buddhism is about cause and effect and by this imply that Buddhism is scientific, the logic of cause and effect in physical science is a zero-sum game. In the world of spirit, however, one and one need not make two, it can make a million. This is because emptiness functions like infinity. It does not obey the one-plus-one rules. It is not three before, therefore three after. How many there are after is a function of the spiritual quality of what went before.

Dharma Master Dogen, to whom we have already made several references, plays on the double meaning of the word *ku*. Ku means emptiness. It also means the sky. Thus, Dogen says that Buddhism is "flowers in the sky". Flowers are manifestations and they naturally lead to fruit. Thus, Buddhism has a kind of cause and effect, but it is unlike the cause and effect of physics. In this cause and effect one and one can make a million.

You will remember that we said earlier that the aim of secularism could be said to be the elimination of flowers in the sky: that is, the demythologisation of our world; but that Dogen says that Buddhism is all a matter of flowers in the sky and that in order to understand Buddhism one has to understand how flowers falling from the sky have palpable effect on the ground.

Buddhism is about the unconditioned. Whereas conditioned actions conform to the logic of one plus one equals two and three before inevitably only leaves three after, unconditioned actions have a logic of their own that bursts the bounds of one plus one and makes it possible to escape from the only world that modernity would have us believe in.

Thus Dharma is a cause and effect in which there is a built-in multiplier. Take, for instance, the bowl of milk rice that Sujata gave to the Buddha. From this small gift came whole civilizations. If she had not gratuitously given this food to the Buddha when he was most in need, he would not have recovered, not have awakened, not have taught and not have transmitted the Dharma. The Buddhist religion would never have been founded and history would have been poorer to an incalculable extent.

Much later in history, the Mongol armies conquered China. When they became overlords of China, the Mongols gave up their animistic religion and took up the Tibetan form of Buddhism. Their conquest included the besieging and taking of Beijing, which, at that time, was, perhaps, the most heavily fortified city in the world. Inside Beijing, at the time of the siege, a Buddhist retreat was held. In that retreat was a man called Yelui Chu Tsai. During this period of intensive practice in rather extreme circumstances, Yelui had a great experience of spiritual awakening. When the Mongols finally took the city, they made an audit of the population to see who was useful to them. Yelui had been a civil servant in the government and so was a literate man. He was also a person of the Khitan race. The Khitan were a subject people of the Chinese. Yelui was selected as one of those to be interviewed by Gengis Khan himself. The Khan liked to interview the most interesting captives. He was always interested in what he could learn.

Gengis said to Yelui, "You, as a Khitan, cannot be altogether displeased that the Chinese have been defeated at last."

Yelui replied, "Sire, it would be improper for me to speak ill of my former employers."

This was a bold thing to say in the circumstances. Many of the people Gengis interviewed ended up executed.

Gengis was impressed. Yelui clearly had an upright character and manifested a fearlessness that was, in fact, the fruit of his spiritual awakening. Spiritual awakening means that one loses one's sense of self-interest. Gengis made Yelui a minister in his new government.

The Mongols had to decide what to do with the big country they had now conquered. Many thought that the best idea was to exterminate the Chinese and use the land for rearing horses. Yelui, however, argued that "dead men pay no taxes" and persuaded the Mongols to become overlords rather than genocidists.

In their new enthusiasm for Tibetan Buddhism, the Mongols were inclined to destroy the Confucian and Taoist shrines and temples, but Yelui argued for the value of diversity and balance. Yelui was an honest man who exercised compassion in the midst of a situation where much killing and cruelty was going on. When he died he left no fortune, merely a few musical instruments. He was not corrupt.

We can see, therefore, that the bowl of rice milk that Sujata gave to Siddhartha not only gave rise to Buddhism, it also saved Taoism and Confucianism from destruction as well.

Something from Nothing

In his writing called *Flowers in the Sky*, Eihei Dogen[1] says that the person of ordinary mind thinks that flowers in the sky are a product of having a clouded mind, that unclouding the mind is the task to be achieved, and,

---

[1] In this section, references are to KuGe, which is chapter 43 at pages 9-21 of volume three in the Nishijima & Cross translation of *Master Dogen's Shobogenzo*, published by Windbell Publications, London & Tokyo, 1997

therefore, such a person looks for a technique or procedure by which such unclouding can be accomplished. This is the common approach to spiritual practice. It is spiritual materialism: the importing of the logic of physics into religion.

Buddhism has often been presented in the West in this way. People engage in it as a way of getting something. They understand that what they get out will be in proportion to what they put in. If there are “three before” there will be “three after”. Therefore, they work hard at whatever practice they decide is efficacious. This may be meditation or keeping to a certain discipline or reciting the name of a Buddha or a scripture or whatever. Such people do indeed get a reward that is proportional to what they put in. This, however, is not religion and it is not Buddhadharma.

When there is Buddhadharma there is no thought of getting anything out and yet the sky and the ground are covered with unsought flowers. When there is Buddhadharma everything is done purely on a basis of faith in the beauty of intrinsic goodness. It does not matter, particularly, if it is meditation, or chanting, or offering a bowl of milk rice, or saving a Confucian temple, or taking flowers home for one's spouse. Scale vanishes. Love is not measurable. Generosity is not trade. Compassion cannot be bought. Sympathy cannot be legislated. Nor can their effect be calculated. These flowers in the sky fall to earth in their own way in their own time and do so abundantly when least expected.

This is already true. This is not a truth that needs to be manufactured. Buddhism certainly is belief in cause and effect, but it is not cause and effect of the three before can only make three after variety.

Fuyo Reikun asked, "What is Buddha?"

Dharma Master Kisu Chijo said, "If I tell you, will you believe me or not?"

Reikun replied, "How could I not believe the Master's honest words?"

"You yourself are just it."

"How should I maintain it?"

"When an instance of cloudedness is there in the eyes, flowers in space tumble down."

The worldly mind thinks this is a question of how to possess and maintain cloud free eyes. However, when there is cloudiness, flowers tumble down all around. If Reikun had believed the master's words, then he would not have been anxious about maintaining something. He thinks he believes, but he does not. His eyes are clouded. Flowers are falling, nonetheless.

We think that there is something to grasp and once grasped it must be maintained. However, that is not it. We all have clouded eyes most of the time. Even if the sky clears and we look up at a clear blue heaven, tomorrow there will be cloud again. Nonetheless, flowers fall. We think that our job is to clear the heaven of clouds, but all that is needed is faith in the falling of flowers. Our very efforts to clear the sky make us blind to flowers falling. Whether the clouds are in our eyes or in the sky above makes no difference. There will always be clouds and they have a beauty of their own when in the light.

A truly good person does not do good things out of a calculation of reward. Their goodness is embedded in their faith. A religion provides a wealth of support for such faith. It touches the core of a person. A religion is not a hobby nor is it a means. A person who bargains with God is a person of insecure faith. When God is GOD, there is no bargaining. When Buddha is BUDDHA, one is loved infinitely. There is no judgement. It is not by one's own power and one does not have to maintain such love because it flows from a source inexhaustible. The religious spirit may be wrapped up in different language, but its absolute nature remains the same.

Buddhism is a way of relating to the absolute and that way is pre-eminently faith. From the absolute come riches newly created, unearned, unmade, unconditioned. If this were not so, there would be no liberation and no awakening. When this faith is awakened, one becomes a "gateless gate."

Dharma Master Sekimon Eketsu was asked *"What is the jewel in the mountain?"* This question is equivalent to what it is that one finds through practising meditation. To sit in meditation is to be like a mountain. The purpose of such sitting is assumed to be to find something inside oneself. Hence, *what is the jewel in the mountain?* means *"What is the goal?"* or "*What should I be looking for inside myself?*" or, ultimately, *"What is Buddha?"* The master answered, *"Flowers in space unfold on the ground. Even if we buy throughout the country, there is no gate."* What does this mean?

Dogen comments: Ordinary teachers in many districts when discussing flowers in space as flowers of emptiness speak only of arising in emptiness and passing in emptiness. None has understood reliance on space; how much less could any understand reliance on the ground. Only Sekimon has understood.

In other words, there are many people who discourse on emptiness and talk about the emptiness of phenomena and tell us that Buddhism teaches the essential emptiness of all things, but none of them see how Buddhism is about *relying* upon this emptiness. To rely upon emptiness is faith. They do not understand that this refers to unconditional action, to love and so on. They do not see how spirit affects action amongst concrete things and how action amongst concrete things affects spirit. To understand the Dharma, the fundamental, one must unhook oneself from worldly calculation and from materialist thinking. The basic principle of Buddhism can be said to be that something comes out of nothing. The action that comes out of nothing, which is to say, one that is unconditional, is the heart of the matter. By teaching for forty five years Shakyamuni did not gain anything material, but by smiling for a moment he received unlimited spiritual blessings which he had no use for other than to give them away.

To live by faith is to ask for nothing. Religion is to live in gratitude for blessings already bestowed, providence that enfolds and grace that will surely flow in the future, but which will do so in its own time and in its own way. When one has such faith one is on the great highway or riding in the great vehicle. When one does not have such faith one is trudging through the desert.

Love that is true is unconditional. Unconditional action partakes of the absolute, of what Buddhism calls the other shore (*paramita*). Buddhism, therefore, distinguishes between ordinary virtue and "other shore" virtue, between *dana*, which means generosity, and *dana paramita,* between *kshanti*, patience, and *kshanti paramita*, and so on. The difference lies in whether or not there is an idea of self or gain or achievement in the heart of the doer. Dana paramita is not one's own capacity for generosity, it is the result in oneself of recognising the great generosity that come to one from the other shore. When we appreciate how much we receive, giving becomes natural. It ceases to be a contrivance. It happens unconsciously. Such unconscious action generates unlimited merit without the doer even knowing about it. Nonetheless, even ordinary *dana* reflects the light of *dana paramita*. The reason that we are touched by receiving a gift is not really our material gain, it is the love that we perceive in the act and even ordinary love speaks of ultimate love.

For this reason, the effect of any act of love is out of proportion to the effects attributable to the material act or gift. Love, faith, generosity and so on, are like falling without a parachute. There is no knowing the extent of the possible outcome. The gift of a handful of sand may be the cause of a Buddha appearing in the world.

We should be able to see from this that the cause and effect that we are talking about here is one in which something appears out of emptiness. Emptiness means emptiness of greed, hate and delusion. The more pure the love is the more empty it is. The more empty it is the greater the effect. The less there is before the more there is after. The greatest contributions to the world come out of complete emptiness. That which does not come out of emptiness contributes less.

9: Siddhartha Woke Up

Spiritual Crises are Existential

Siddhartha Gotama was brought up as a prince. He enjoyed luxury and he learnt to be a warrior. Nonetheless, he was a sensitive person, touched by instances of suffering that he observed, several of which notable incidents involved the suffering of non-human creatures: a swan downed in a hunt, worms and beetles turned out of the earth by the plough. He pondered the meaning of it all.

His young life must have must have been powerfully marked by the fact that his birth had caused the death of his mother so that he was brought up by his mother's sister who was also a wife of his father. At some point this constellation of factors crystallised into a spiritual problem. He became acutely aware of the existential challenge posed by the inevitability of aging, disease and death. At this point he saw a holy man and was inspired to enter upon a spiritual path.

This is the general form of religious conversion. People often find faith and direction in life either through seeing the expectations that they formerly had had crumble, or through encountering some inspiring example that shows them what is possible, or some combination of the two. It is seeing the worthlessness of the worldly attitude and seeing an alternative that makes faith possible. Another dimension of this same dynamic is seeing the frailty of oneself, yet, at the same time, realising one's participation in a dispensation much grander than one's own powers could ever encompass.

In the last chapter, we saw Master Sekimon refer to "buying throughout the country." This can refer to collecting spiritual practices, but it can also refer to the fact that it is the ubiquitous, existential facts of life that precipitate us into our spiritual crisis or koan. The universal koan arises from the fact that one is not a special case in relation to these existential realities. We tend to go through life thinking, "It will not happen to me," but, sooner or later, the reality of mortality is borne in upon us. If the only recourse we have at such a time is selfish calculation, we then experience life as empty and meaningless and spend the rest of our time warding off despair. Only by the kind of greater vision that is worthy of the name religious are we lifted at such times into a bigger meaning. It was seeing the holy man that rescued Siddhartha at this point, in just such a way.

The upshot of this crisis was that he left home. He went on a spiritual search. He went to see the best spiritual teachers he could find. He learnt what they had to teach him, but he was not satisfied. He learnt techniques for entering states of bliss, but this did not answer the questions that nagged at his heart. With some friends he started practising religious disciplines independently. Even this was not good enough for him. Eventually he went off on his own. At this time he was dedicated to asceticism. As a psychologist I can see this as a phase of self-punishment and I can speculate that if a person punishes himself he must feel guilty and, in this case, the

most obvious cause of guilt would be the fact that his birth had resulted in his mother's death.

Reflecting in this way we can see Siddhartha's koan unfolding in two main stages. The first stage brought him up against the existential limits, birth, disease, old age and death. If we are nothing more than this, it seems like a tragedy. If one is a tragic figure then, in a society that believes in karma, one must be guilty, and, indeed, he could see himself as guilty. Of course, our lives have all caused other deaths: even the harvesting of vegetarian food generally results in the deaths of some creatures, not to mention our participation in the expansion of our species at the expense of other ones, or of our country at that of others. We are the fruit of struggles and conquests. The world is made that way. There is no escape. The attempt to be personally pure when in a world such as this is vain. When the death one has occasioned is one's own mother, however, the impact will be particularly sharp and deluding oneself in the way that most people do will be particularly difficult.

Conceit having been cracked in this way, Siddhartha sought to restore the karmic balance by punishing himself. One way or another, the guilty seek punishment. In due course he seems to have reached rock bottom. Having rejected his family, his prospects of a kingdom, his wife and child, his teachers and his friends and punished himself until he was so starved that his ribs stood out, he was at an extremity. At this point a passing woman called Sujata took pity on him and nurtured him back to health. This maternal, compassionate intervention had a profound effect upon him. In short order he turned his life around and emerged inspired by a new perspective that became the foundation of a teaching career spanning the next five decades.

This turnaround can be characterised in several ways. We can understand it psychologically, but this understanding, while not false, does not go the whole way to explaining the impact that Siddhartha's new understanding had on his life and on the whole world. Again, his new understanding had an intellectual content, called the theory of dependent origination, but the element of personal liberation involved was more crucial. Dependent origination explained delusion, but what the new Buddha was interested in was liberation from such delusion. Reducing what happened to him to its elements does not give us the meaning. The meaning lies in how he opened up to a larger sense of what life was about. Before his enlightenment he was obsessed with himself and his own needs; after it he was concerned about all sentient beings and the meaning of life.

He now realised that self-punishment was simply a different kind of conceit. If all one's energy is given to a spiritual practice, it is because, at some level, one thinks that what happens to and in oneself is the most important thing in all the world. It is not. Buddha did not wake up to the necessity to do this or that particular practice. He awoke to the necessity to understand deeply that this conditioned life only becomes meaningful through a relationship to the unconditioned.

The core of Siddhartha Gotama's awakened vision, therefore, was a realisation of how blind the ordinary person is and also of release from that blindness, coupled with a realisation that such blindness is a manifestation of conceit. He understood how such conceit functions in ordinary life to keep a person going round in fruitless circles of the "three before makes three after" kind. The essential element in dependent origination is the delusion producing effect of self-seeking. Our contemporary society is substantially founded on a philosophy of individual and collective self-seeking that valorises accumulation, material gain and personal indulgence and convenience and it, therefore, represents exactly the kind of outlook that Buddhism exists to rescue people from. Although there has been a powerful movement toward producing a "modern Buddhism" that accommodates, or even conforms to, the values of our time, fundamentally, the Buddhist project aims in a completely different direction.

Buddha said that the period that he spent doing ascetic practice was "vain, ignoble and useless". It was vain because it did not produce spiritual result. It was ignoble because it was self-centred. It was useless because it helped nobody. Yet, many people, especially in the West, who consider themselves Buddhist, are actually engaged in copying Siddhartha's mistake rather than learning from his experience. They vainly devote themselves to practices, many of which are boring or painful, in a self-centred project to get some supposedly spiritual reward, a personal release or self-justification, that will pay off their karmic debt.

Our karmic debt is actually so vast that it is impossible to pay off on a "three before makes three after" basis. One cannot earn salvation; one cannot make it or own it, any more than one can earn, manufacture or own the sunshine that falls on the virtuous and sinners alike. Nirvana is unconditioned. We may think that we can create the conditions necessary to yield nirvana, but this is actually a contradiction of terms.

Ultimately, Buddhism is not about accumulation, neither of merit, nor practice hours, nor intellectual understandings, nor anything. Nor is it a matter of membership, of being one of the in-crowd who have the right doctrine, or the right practice, or the right logo, or the biggest membership list. None of these ways of thinking can have anything in common with Buddhadharma as Buddha understood it when he awoke.

If you calculate karmic debt on a one-for-one, three-for-three, basis, then the blessings that one has received will always vastly outweigh any good that one has done. How can I possibly repay the debt I owe to all the life forms that I have eaten, to all the people in history who have created the technology and civilisation that I as a modern person take for granted, to my mother who cared for me in infancy and loved me throughout her life? How many people have contributed to me being able to sit here in a centrally heated building writing on a state of the art computer? On a three-for-three basis, we are all so deeply in debt that it is hopeless to think of ever getting out of the red.

What to do When one Wakes up

Siddhartha woke up. He saw that what he had been devoting his life to was a self-centred project. He conceived a revulsion for it. His life turned around, yet his first thought was, "Nobody is going to understand this."

At this point a god appeared. Brahma Sahampati persuaded him to go forth and teach. *There will be a few with little dust in their eyes, who are wasting through not hearing the Dharma.*

Thus, following divine persuasion, Gotama went forth to teach. He thought of his former teachers, but realised by supernatural awareness that they had died. He thought of his former companions and set out to find them. On the way he met a holy man of another persuasion. They conversed. Gotama told the man about his own awakening. The man was sceptical, "That may be so," he said, politely, and went his way. Then Gotama met two travelling merchants. They recognised Gotama as a Buddha and took refuge. They took refuge in Buddha and Dharma. They were the first two people to have faith in the new religion. Their awakening came from meeting the Buddha. He did not teach them a method. He acknowledged their faith. At this point, apart from Buddha himself, there were two Buddhists in the world. They were lay people and they were Buddhist because they had faith. They had taken refuge.

Then he found his former companions and taught them the discourses that are called "Setting in Motion the Wheel of the Dharma" and "The Discourse on Non-self". These five then became the first renunciant disciples. The Buddha then travelled to other places and acquired more disciples and more faith-followers. Soon he had sixty disciples. He sent them forth to teach all over the country. This was the founding of the Buddhist religion, an organised spiritual mission to the people. India being a monsoon country, the disciples adopted the practice of going forth in ones, twos and small groups in the dry season and gathering together in the wet season. The faith-followers made it their business to facilitate these travels and retreats. It was no small operation. An organised spirituality is a religion. It very soon has rules, conventions, stories, symbols, holy days, disciplines, pastoral care, retreats, initiations, and gatherings. There has to be organisation of catering, sleeping arrangements, lecture spaces, discussion groups, and times for collective community activities. It was probably the first renunciant order to be so well organised and the relationship between the lay faithful and the renunciants ensured a dynamic life to the whole community. Thus the great vision was sustained and transmitted and in due course millions found faith. When Buddha woke up he created a religion. This was a gift to the world and it is still in being, still bearing flowers and fruit.

There is plenty of evidence in his later utterances that although he did see himself as having made a unique contribution to spirituality in his generation, he also saw himself as participating in a great lineage stretching back into the past and forward into the future into barely conceivable extensions of time. He met the *tathagatas* of the three times. "Three times" means past, present and future, i.e. all time. Tathagata can be construed as meaning one who has gone to, or come from, *tatha*. Tatha, literally "such-ness," is virtually untranslatable, but refers to ultimate reality. As our friend Dogen says, *ultimately it is all just Buddhas together with Buddhas*.

I think it is important that we emphasise the vastness of this vision. I do not think that Shakyamuni could have done what he did, or been what he was, without a great vision of his and our place in the scheme of things. This great vision makes his role religious and means that it cannot, on its own terms, be reduced merely to psychology. It can dialogue with modernity, but it cannot be part of it.

In a sense deeper than the commonplace, there is no modern Buddhism, no American Buddhism, no European Buddhism. There is Buddhism in modern times, Buddhism in America and Buddhism in Europe, but the Dharma is not a function of culture. It is something that expresses itself through cultures, but, in itself, it is deeper and vaster than any of the cultures it has dealings with. One day there might be a Buddhist America or a Buddhist Europe or a Buddhist modernity, but if this were ever to come to pass then that America, that Europe or that modernity would have undergone a profound transformation from the ones that we see today.

Buddha developed particular social forms, all the forms that make up the social manifestation of a religion, but he did so in order to reveal the Dharma, which is a fundamental that gives one a deep and reverential feel for life and truth that is beyond the mundane.

Buddhism does not need to create a Buddhist America or a Buddhist Europe. Buddha was not interested in hegemony. He was interested in profound, religious truth. The Dharma can and does find expression in other religions. Let us pray that our gods be Buddhas.

We will not understand this while we continue to think that what is needed is to make Buddhism popular by fitting it into worldly categories. Our best chance is to realise that Buddhism is a religion and let ourselves go into the free-fall that such a realisation will precipitate us into. It is more than just *a* religion. It is Dharma which is the awakening to the foundation of all religion. It is this foundation that makes life meaningful and allows us to transcend our limited existential plight.

Birth, disease, old age and death: this is our lot; yet, we can have faith in our participation in a life vast and eternal, a love unconditional, a dispensation that is universally salvific, not just for the few, but for all sentient beings, for Buddhists of all religions.

Siddhartha had such a vision and set about propagating it. He gathered disciples. He converted other teachers who then brought their disciples along. His followers organised retreats and gatherings for teaching. They organised, educated, activated and spread the word. This caused a considerable social upheaval. Young people left home to go and join the Buddha, sometimes against fierce opposition from their parents. Some who could not gain parental approval went on hunger strike until they were allowed to go. In India in those days, religion was regarded as something to devote oneself to in old age. The Buddha, on the other hand, led large numbers of young people to reject the established conventions and go forth in a great movement to change the values of the world, from violence to peace, from accumulation to sharing, from selfishness to faith. The movement had opponents and supporters. Buddha often had to argue his case.

Pietistic tradition would have it that once Shakyamuni was enlightened he knew everything that he needed to know and was immune to making mistakes. From then on it was a matter simply of distributing the teaching. This is almost certainly an erroneous view. His awakening gave him faith, but it did not give him all the answers. Firstly, he had to go back and sort out the mess he had left behind in his family. Then he had to visit heaven and make peace with his dead mother. Then he had all the problems of organisation that come with a growing movement. Should they admit women, in the face of strong social pressure to the contrary? Surely the Buddha had already caused trouble enough: if he admitted women to the religious life this would undermine the family in a fundamental way. So people thought. Initially Buddha resisted admitting women, but then he changed his mind. When we reflect on the fact that Buddha was initially disinclined to teach and had to be persuaded by a god and was disinclined to admit women and then changed his mind in the course of a conversation with Ananda who was not enlightened, we see that spiritual awakening was not a matter of becoming infallible. Buddha went on learning, changing, growing and evolving. It was his new faith that enabled him to do so. If we think of awakening as some kind of infallibility this will not make any sense. However, if we see that the essence of awakening is faith, it makes perfect sense. The person who has faith is open to whatever will help to put that faith into practice. He is not defending his own ego. He has a higher purpose. Along the way he will make mistakes and as he sees them he will change course. Over his lifetime Buddha also changed some of the rules and conventions of his community, sometimes more than once, and he certainly changed his style of teaching in order to reach different groups of people and people at different stages of spiritual development. Real faith is thus.

The faith to which Siddhartha awoke enabled him to see beyond superficial appearances. He could read what was in a person's heart. He could not be bribed or manipulated because he was not defending his own ego.

On one occasion he said that one should not get angry when others are critical of oneself because if you do you will not be able to see what parts of what the person says are true and what parts are not.

Horizontal and Vertical

There is something further to say about the effect of having the Unborn always in mind. We have seen how at the materialist level there is calculation. There is gain and loss and there is comparison. In a materialist life everything is hierarchical. Things are on vertical scales. The materialist wants to be richer, higher status, more handsome or whatever. Always it is a competition, a race, a ladder to climb. Materialism is verticalism.

In the absolute, there is no calculation. Calculation makes no sense. Buddha loves everybody. It does not matter if they are good or bad, high or low, old or young, the love is total in every case. There can be no comparison. Nothing is on a vertical scale. The awakening of one who has accessed the Unborn puts everything onto a horizontal plane. In the absolute, there is no gain, no loss, no coming, no going, no birth, no death.

In the spiritual in-between, these two mix. From a spiritual point of view there is calculation: some things are better than others - kindness is better than killing, generosity is better than theft, and so on, yet, in the back of these choices there lies an awareness of that nirvana where even the thief and the killer are objects of the same unconditional love and no one is better, no one worse.

After his awakening, Siddhartha had the right mix of such spiritual and absolute perspectives. He wanted his monks to be worthy: to be beyond reproach. At the same time, his compassion encompassed everyone. There are numerous stories of him refusing to prioritise higher status people over lower status ones even where the low status was because the person was a prostitute or a criminal.

The spiritual life, therefore, involves both the vertical and the horizontal. The vertical, however, is the spiritual vertical, not the worldly, materialist vertical, and the horizontal is the real foundation. This latter culminates in what Buddhists call the consummate vision (*sama-dhi*) of equality. In the consummate vision itself, even the idea of progression loses all meaning.

Religion is about how we relate to the absolute and that includes how, stuck here as we are in this world of relativities, we relate to the absolute ultimate equality of all being. To do so directly is a rare mystical experience. To do so day to day is to keep such experience in mind as it percolates through the actual practical life that we have, perforce, to live.

In practice, this is done in a religious manner. The devotee realises that he or she is not capable of always seeing the world through the eyes of unconditional love in which all are worthy. However, this devotee has faith in Buddha. Buddha, being metaphysical, has precisely such an unconditional love. This unconditional love of Buddha is more real than the empirical, partial love that one encounters reflected here on the ground of *samsara* (the ordinary world). The Buddhist devotee is somebody who keeps Buddha reverently in mind. When a difficult situation comes up, he or she prays to Buddha for help. This means that they bring up the awareness that even though one may, oneself, fail to find wisdom or compassion in a particular situation, one has faith that such compassion and wisdom do exist. They are not here in the transient empirical world, perhaps. They might be absent from one's own heart at a particular moment, or in a particular constellation of conditions, but one has faith that they exist in the heart of Buddha. It is in this that a Buddhist places faith and it is this faith that rescues one, even in the most dire of circumstances. One can be helped.

10: Worship in Buddhism

Buddhists have always worshipped. A Buddhist temple is generally set up with this purpose primarily in mind. When we look at Christian churches we see various different styles. In the older traditions such as Orthodox, Catholic or High Church, the centre of attention is the altar. Around the altar is an area where especial reverence is expected. These religious traditions are centred on the mystery and their rites generally have a mystical element which is normally taken to be the most important dimension of what is happening. The ritual of such a temple is a kind of sacred theatre. When the priest enters the holy space he does so on behalf of all of us. When we enter the space we feel a special reverence. This is how such religion works.

It is a very ancient approach. One finds the same in shamanism, for instance. The shaman may draw a circle on the ground. Within that circle things happen that are not ordinary. A sacred space has been created into which the spirit or spirits will come. When one enters such a zone one enters a slightly or greatly altered state of consciousness in which one is more open to the influence of that power that transcends, or comes from outside of ordinary mundane life.

In the traditions of more recent origin, such as some of the Protestant or Non-conformist churches, the centre of attention is not the altar but the pulpit. These churches are dominated by words and explanation. It is a more rationalist approach. We have probably all visited churches of both types and if you have not and want to check it out you have only to walk into town and visit a few places of worship. In Leicester in England where I used to live the contrast between the Anglican cathedral of the former type and the Methodist church of the latter was very striking. In the oldest cathedrals, too, the architecture is such that it is possible to circumambulate the holy area around the altar. If you go to an old cathedral such as Tewkesbury in England or Chartres in France you can walk all the way around. The holy area contains, in addition to the altar, the tombs of saints and important persons from the past. By circumambulating one can show respect, gather the holy energy emanating from that sacred place, and feel oneself in the presence of God and the saints. This is how that kind of religion functions. Some people might say that "God does not live in buildings," and this has a grain of truth. In fact, historically, such practice did not begin in buildings at all. It was originally done outside. Our stone age ancestors and even the ancient Greeks all worshipped outdoors. The tradition of circumambulating the holy place, which is often also the place where the relics of holy beings are kept, is extremely ancient. Putting a roof over the practice must have grown up as a convenience.

The practice of circumambulation is rooted in archetypal forms. It is deep in our being. Whenever I drive past Stonehenge there are always people doing the circular walk around it. They are not all druids. Many consider themselves to be nothing more than tourists, but all gain something by doing this apparently irrational act of prescribing a magic circle or mandala with their own steps around the place that has been a centre of devotion for thousands of years. Unconsciously they are enacting a form of prayer. In the Buddhist texts it frequently describes how people showed respect for the Buddha by walking around him before they sat down. Walking around somebody in a clockwise direction demonstrates trust. It shows that there is no intention to do harm, no weapon in the right hand, no wrong action when one is behind the back of the seated teacher. Buddhist monks even traditionally wore robes in which the left shoulder and arm are completely bare which demonstrates an absence of weapons. This is about demonstrating peace and respect, and establishing a space of tranquillity and reverence. These things are deeply embedded in us.

When we consider Buddhist temples they are of the mystical type. The focus of attention is the altar. If there is anything resembling a pulpit it is subordinate to the altar or shrine. Sometimes the altar is constructed in such a way that you can walk around it, sometimes not, but there is little doubt, when you walk into such a hall, where the centre of energy is. There is likely to be a figure of a Buddha, often on a high pedestal. Around it will be all manner of symbolic objects representing the holy realm or other holy beings. Altars in Buddhist temples are often much more elaborate even than in other religions. All this is part of the mystery. It creates a sacred space. Such halls are primarily for worship and for being in the holy presence. In some Western countries practitioners of meditation have created a new, plainer style in which there are no images and, perhaps, not even an altar, but this is something new, an attempt to impose a different philosophy on Buddhism, depriving it of its mystical depth. The people who create such places are partly catering to secular taste and partly to a belief that traditional form is somehow an aberration. My contention in this book is that this is a mistake. It is the modern secular style that is an innovation, out of keeping with the original intention.

When a Buddhist enters a temple hall, he or she is going into a place where they feel the presence of the Buddha, the spiritual ancestors and all the holy beings. This is a metaphysical presence. The beings are not there in the flesh. The devotions that the practitioner expresses are addressed to the holy beings and these beings are celestial. This is not an aberration. This is the normal substance of real Buddhist practice. By going to the shrine one exposes oneself to the influence of the power of the holy. This influence enters one's life, soothing personal inner conflicts and empowering one with an energy and a peace that one then takes forth into the world. This power is something that one receives. It is not one's own creation.

Many temples also have a shrine area devoted to our worldly ancestors. Devotees come and add tokens of the deceased. On anniversaries of the death, the stele of the person who has passed on is brought out and a ritual takes place to honour the memory, but also to effect an exchange with the dead person. The living hope to bring peace to their ancestor and also hope that the influence of the ancestor will continue to be benevolent in their own lives.

These are thoroughly religious procedures. Buddhist worship is commonly performed with all the apparatus of religion involved. Devotees make offerings of food, water, candles, incense, music, and other gifts. They kneel and prostrate. They sit with hands in the attitude of prayer. They allow the power of Buddha to enter their minds. We do not need to be ashamed of this. Ritual and prayer are fundamental, age-old human activities of vital importance. The forms that they employ are deeply rooted in our being and speak to a part of us that is barely touched by rational words and explanations. The core of Buddhist practice is not the pulpit and the Dharma talk, valuable as that may sometimes be, but the direct encounter between the practitioner and the spirit of Buddha, which is deemed to be eternal and universally accessible, though especially so in sacred places established for the purpose. The main function of a Dharma talk is simply to share, or encourage, such encounter. The idea that receiving the Dharma is a matter of understanding an intellectual presentation of information is well wide of the mark. Buddhism has always supported and been in favour of education and science, but in Buddhism these are not seen as opposed to, or alternative to, religion, they are simply extensions of it. Religion gives depth and direction to life. Science and education help us in our expression of that depth through practical action in the world.

Buddhists may engage in any of the various forms of prayer - petitionary, confessatorial, devotional, and so on – but the core is refuge. This is a mystical act. Some contemporary Buddhist groups have substituted such phrases as “I go to the Buddha for guidance” but this is a watering down. Certainly, a Buddhist prays to receive guidance from the Buddha, but refuge is more than just guidance.

Why does one go for refuge? Because the body is unreliable, the emotions are unreliable, the mind is unreliable and the world is on fire with greed, hate and delusion. This is the core of Buddha's teaching. Contemporary popular spirituality tells us that our bodies are a source of wisdom or that we should rely upon our feelings or that our own mind encompasses the whole of existence or that everything comes from within ourselves and that we do not need anything beyond self. These ideas are popular and each points to something of value. It is useful for our corporeal being to be grounded, but the body will eventually let us down and even day to day it is rarely completely at peace. It is informative to pay attention to our feelings, but feelings are blown about by all the winds of changing circumstance that blow through our lives. The mind is a mirror of crucial importance and Buddhism is in favour of mind training and advances some of the most sophisticated approaches to this art, but in the end Buddhism is not fundamentally about mind control because the mind is like a troop of monkeys. One can discipline them to a degree, one can exploit their creativity too, but ultimately one has to accept that one's mind is an unreliable basis for ultimate knowledge and often enough makes mistakes in quite ordinary matters. We all know this intuitively and the worldly solution is to try to anchor oneself in circumstance or relationships, but, again, the Buddha points out that the world is on fire with passion and one can easily be burnt. With all of these taken away, what remains? Such consideration plunges us into the kind of reflection that can only be called mystical. Formally,

Buddhism says, "Take refuge!" Take refuge in Buddha, in Dharma, and in Sangha.

Here again the modern tendency has been to redefine sangha as ourselves, the participants in the Buddhist enterprise. Thus we end up taking refuge in ourselves. This, however, is not what refuge meant originally. The sangha of refuge is the presence of holy beings past, present and future. It is a metaphysical reality. Human beings may eventually pass into this entity insofar as they have lived and embodied the Dharma. They become exemplars.

The core of Buddhist prayer is refuge. No matter what else is happening...

To the Buddha for refuge I am going
To the Dharma for refuge I am going
To the Sangha for refuge I am going

The substance of the objects of refuge, however, is metaphysical. In Buddhism the divide between the two worlds is paper thin. The holy is not remote, but it is distinct.

Religion exists when there is a division between the sacred and the mundane, said the famous sociologist Emile Durkheim in his study of the elements of the religious life. This is a good definition. Much modern thinking has sought to demolish this distinction, or to eliminate the sacred from our lives. Again, some contemporary spiritualities see their task as to demolish the duality in the opposite way by making everything sacred. However, the spiritual life always has as its central focus an awareness of the holy and of the fact that not everything is holy.

All religion is thus. Some claim that Buddhism, Taoism and, perhaps, Confucianism are exceptions, but historically that is not the case. Some modernised presentations have sought to strip these ancient paths of anything spiritual in order to make them accord with secular rationalism, but in the process they are depotentiated. The power of the spiritual life lies precisely in the fact that it is centred upon the beyond; upon what is not oneself, out of reach of one's ego. The spirit is in the world, but not of the world.

It is the tension between me and my world on the one hand and something else that is more than I am that generates the dynamic that powers the religious quest. Prayer is meaningless without this sense of the presence of something more. Different systems frame this non-self principle differently, with varying metaphysics and mythology, but the fundamental principle that spirituality is a calling from within the prison of the ego to what is beyond holds in all cases. The Zen philosopher Eihei Dogen says that although the nature of Buddha is the nature of the totality of being, one will not know the nature of Buddha until one realises that one is without the nature of Buddha. This is like saying that although God is All, you will not know God until you know that you are not God. Ultimately, this is to know that you are nothing, empty, shunyata.

For a life to be spiritual means that it is focussed upon something that is more important than the ego. Adding the idea of a Self with a capital "S" achieves nothing in this respect. The greatest obstacle to spiritual progress is concern for oneself and the centring of all one's thought constellation upon one's ego complex. Buddhism is no different from other religions in this respect. In fact, Buddhism goes further than most with a refined development of thought on the subject of emptiness and transcendence.

Modern “spirituality” as well as much other contemporary thinking has tended to be ego-worship, and it is not uncommon for contemporary Buddhist discourse to adopt some of the language of this way of thinking, but when it does so it is very easy to slip from apologetics into a complete corruption of the original message which is self-denying not self-affirming.

Buddha tells us that there is a counter to self-obsession and that this contrary focus actually has much greater liberating power than the ego can ever have. The simplest and most direct appeal to this contrary focus is taking refuge. It is precisely this that gives the holy life its potency. It is the amplifier that makes us radiant.

The Dharma is rare and difficult to encounter even in a thousand million years, Now we can see, hear and receive it. We pray that we may be able to receive the Tathagata's true meaning.

The Dharma is not just words. We see it. We encounter it. How? Where? In holy places and in holy people. Those who are already infected with this charism are an inspiration to others. Those who make the Dharma their light, themselves become a light in the world. This is not by the power of their own selves. The simplest way of thinking of it is that the power of the Buddhas flows through such people. They are inspired. Buddhism is subtle and tells us that although the power of the Buddhas flows through there is no thing that flows through. This power is not something that we could reduce to materialistic categories. It is most real nonetheless. Buddhism is an invitation to wake up to it.

This is what Buddha brought to the world and what his disciples have transmitted. We can see this from the fact that many people caught it from Buddha and have been transmitting it ever since. All who truly do so thereby become “eternal Buddhas”. The secular way is to try to make everything physical, or reduce it to a protocol that could be administered by anybody who follows the instructions. However, meeting the Dalai Lama is not just meeting anybody who wears those clothes and says those words. Those who carry the charism of Buddha are infectious. It is good to see such sages. We are benefitted. When they are not physically present we pray that they may be metaphysically so. We pray that they may stay in the world, revolving the Dharma wheel, until samsara ceases. We express our gratitude which is limitless and receive their equally limitless blessing. This is religion and it is what Buddha brought and taught.

I have heard people say, “Buddha wasn't a Buddhist. He was not trying to start a religion.” This is, basically, just not true. Jesus was not a Christian, perhaps. It took St Paul to make Christianity, though Jesus was teaching religion. He saw himself as reforming and purifying the religion of his time and place. Buddha, however, was definitely a religious organiser. He created a church. Many of the things that we now think of as constituting significant elements of religion such as an order of monks with a clear rule of conduct and regular confession ceremonies go back directly to Buddha. Buddha lived in a world of cults and reformed them into a religion. Far from Buddhism not being a religion, much of what we call religion had its origin with Buddha. As Buddhists, therefore, we should not be shy of using religious forms and the logic of religion, including the logic of prayer.

Prayer springs from the longing in our hearts. I, an ordinary being, conscious of my own numberless shortcomings, call out to the spiritual conquerors, the saints, the fully enlightened ones to come to my aid. Buddhists have been saying words to this effect ever since the religion began.

Many modern people hate the idea of praying and worshipping. They do not want anything to be mightier than themselves. They want to reframe the whole matter in a self-centric form. They will say, "When you bow to the Buddha you are bowing to yourself; you are bowing to the Buddha within yourself." When you one day become fully enlightened this might then be so – I would not know – but it is not true now and, more to the point, it is not a useful way to think because it tends toward solipsism and narcissism. A person who can recognise nothing as higher than himself is lost in the very conceit that Buddha laboured so arduously to free us from. It is much more sane and healthy to pray to Buddha with a sense of his otherness, with the idea that from that Other, blessings flow and in that presence I may receive something precious. In order to receive this blessing it is not necessary that I understand the exact nature of the being to whom I am praying. The fact of mystery is also important because it too emphasises the fact that this is more than my ordinary mind can encompass. It is the calling out of the ordinary limited mind toward what is infinite, and therefore ungraspable, that is the essential point.

Buddhism, therefore, is and always has been a mystical religion and it is from that mystic source that all its myriad treasures flow. Just as in the physical universe, we do not understand so-called black holes, but we see that our galaxy revolves around one, so in the spiritual world all revolves around a powerful mystery.

11: Transmitting the Dharma

Buddhism is a religion that is transmitted. It passes down through the generations from heart to heart. It thus depends upon relationships. There has grown up, particularly in the West, the idea that because Siddhartha Gotama arrived at enlightenment after a period of ascetic living, while meditating for a night, the way to enlightenment must be to imitate what he did. However, he himself said that the ascetic practice had been "vain, ignoble and useless," and that while he himself had thus been enlightened on his own, to do so was extremely rare even in cosmic time.

Even in the Zen school of Buddhism, which is said to be the one that places most emphasis on meditation and personal striving, when we look at the history of the great teachers of the tradition, few, if any, were enlightened while meditating. They were nearly all enlightened in the course of an interpersonal encounter. It was a relationship that enlightened them.

Similarly, when we look at what happened during the life of Shakyamuni, what we have is mostly a record of his encounters. People came to see the Buddha and asked for guidance, or posed a question. Such questions represent the spiritual problems that people have been wrestling with. Ultimately such questions, or *koans*, are a function of the interaction, and often irreconcilability, between a person's bhavanga and their life experience. Anyway, whatever the origins of the problems, people have them. People came and presented their spiritual dilemmas to Buddha, and he received them, and showed compassion and wisdom, and many people went away touched to the core of their being.

It was through their encounter with Buddha that they experienced a turning around in their heart. We talk about enlightenment and the word suggests, perhaps, something almost intellectual; however, what really changes people is something that touches their hearts. People went away from their meetings with Buddha expressing great joy. "Oh, it is as if a person who was lost in the desert had been found; as if one in prison were set free; as if something that was precious that had got broken were suddenly, magically restored!" This is the kind of joy and alacrity that sprang up in people when, through conversing with Buddha, they understood something that had defeated them for a long time.

People went away from such encounters filled with faith. They took refuge in the Buddha. It is not primarily that they had some new intellectual understanding. They might have had such, but that was not what did the trick, nor what lived with them to revolutionise their life.

Nor were such people necessarily ones who had done much prior spiritual training. Sometimes they were people from another spiritual sect or tradition, and we can assume that they had done a lot of meditation or yogic practice, but this is by no means always the case. Many were ordinary lay people who had come up against the existential problems of life – the death of parents or a child, marital desertion, or madness. Some, such as

Angulimala, the bandit, or Ambapali, the prostitute, were people who had clearly not led morally pure lives. Quite a number were people in high places who must have been involved in wars and politics with all its half truths and machinations.

We do not get a picture from these stories that supports the idea of enlightenment being something that is achieved by many years of disciplined individual practice or even accumulation of virtue. Rather we see a great diversity of people who have come up against the realities of life being released from their inner torment through a close encounter with the all-loving sage. They pick up something of his inspiration.

People found faith when they met the Buddha. Not everybody who spoke to the Buddha went away so inspired. In some cases, the prejudice was too strong or the heart was too closed. When King Ajatashatru comes to see the Buddha they have a profound and touching encounter, and afterwards the disciples comment that they think that the king was deeply affected by what had happened and the Buddha affirms that this is so, but adds that Ajatashatru would have had an even deeper experience were it not that the king had killed his own father.

We can see from this example that different people have different degrees of need and that there can be different degrees of awakening. Also, there is a sense in which people are ripe to varying degrees. When Shakyamuni was dying, he said that those who were ready to "cross over" he had helped across, and those who were not ready would have to await another opportunity. We have already seen how Honen asked himself why he was not one of the ones who was ready at the time of Shakyamuni. Sometimes we have to be modest about our own case.

So, valuable as meditation, ethical behaviour, ritual observance, and so on all are, faith and true refuge is not so much a reward for personal effort or something earned, as it is the fruit of meeting the Buddha and being deeply touched.

We can say that Buddhists are those who have met the Buddha and been seized by his spiritual power. How can we meet the Buddha? It may happen, seemingly miraculously, in an encounter with a sambhogakaya buddha. More commonly, it happens through meeting somebody else who has already been similarly affected. The Buddha's living presence is a transmission, heart to heart. We can meet the Buddha in encounters with those who have already been seized by his inspiring influence through encounters of their own.

Again, we should not jump from this knowledge of how it generally happens to an attempt to systematise. A person who is a teacher for one, may not work for another. Simply because somebody is a famous teacher, it does not follow that they will be the person who will touch your heart. Nor is there any system that will ensure that you can know in advance who is the best teacher for you.

It is like falling in love. You can have all kind of ideas about what kind of person you want to fall in love with, but mostly such ideas only get in the way. They may lead you to ignore or rule out the very person who truly loves you.

There are some wonderful Tibetan stories that illustrate these truths. Thus, Milarepa, one of the greatest teachers of Tibet, was not seeking a spiritual guru at all. Rather he was looking for somebody who could teach him the kind of magic arts that would enable him to get revenge on the people who had cheated him out of his inheritance. Thus he met Marpa, who was a layman living as a farmer, who, nonetheless, had great faith, and had travelled to India and received the Buddhist teachings. Marpa and his wife took young Milarepa in hand and thus Tibet gained a great sage.

Earlier in the same line of transmission, there had been a great pandit, Naropa. A pandit is a learned scholar. Naropa was a cultured man who had learnt as much as the university where he worked could teach him. He still felt that something vital was missing from his understanding. He heard a rumour about a man called Tilopa and instantly, intuitively, he knew that he had to go and find this person who he believed might have something to offer to his condition.

After making enquiries, Naropa found his way to a fishing village. He asked local people if they knew of a Buddhist teacher called Tilopa. "We don't know any great teachers," the villagers said, "but there is a fellow called Tilopa who lives as a beggar down by the pier. He lives off the bits of the fish that we throw away." Thus Naropa found his guru.

Stories such as these give us the realisation that things happen in unique ways according to the peculiar logic of human life with all its diversity and ups and downs. We can grasp that the spiritual path is full of surprises, and the person who is not willing to take risks with their life is unlikely to profit from it. The willingness to take risks is itself a function of faith. The more faith one has the more willing one is to venture out of one's established comfort zone on the chance of encountering something new and important. A basic reason why many people are less enlightened than they might have been is because they are too comfortable.

Most contemporary people in a modern society have worked their way into a position where they are trapped. They are not exactly slaves, but they have created for themselves a situation in which a certain comfort of lifestyle depends upon a quantity of debt to which they are obligated and so they live a regular life that may seem relatively meaningless, existing only in order to create more of the same.

Naropa's new guru made many extreme demands upon him. Shock by shock Naropa was jolted out of the complacent presuppositions upon which he had built his comfortable, respectable life. It is not that a civilised life is a bad thing, it is that we can become spiritually effete by becoming dependent upon it. If we cannot live without hot water on tap, we are unlikely to appreciate what the basic meaning of life has been, or even what actual life has been for millions of people throughout history.

Sudden awakening of faith leads to gradual cultivation of those capacities that make one a free person, as at home in a palace as a cave, a cave as a palace. The awakened person has few desires, yet appreciates all manner of things, knows how much is enough, yet is willing to go beyond all artificial boundaries, is serene yet knows how to have fun and is a joy to be with, has great energy, yet knows how to relax, exudes happiness, yet grieves when it is appropriate to do so. This is the natural fruit of being mindful of one's object of faith when that object itself is wholesome, wise, benign and compassionate.

Does one need a teacher in order to be Buddhist? It is possible that one will become Buddhist through a direct intuition, perhaps when visiting a Buddhist temple or seeing a Buddhist statue, or that one will arrive at conviction of Buddhist teachings through reading and desire to know more, or that one will get hold of a Buddhist practice and employ it faithfully for a long time on one's own. There are any number of ways of participating. However, the real deepening of faith generally comes through relationships. Those who have a kind teacher and a loving spiritual community are fortunate indeed. As with so many things discussed in this book, it is not something one can legislate about, but it is clear that Buddhism is, essentially, a heart to heart transmission and if one finds such a connection it is something to treasure eternally.

12: Meeting a Pure Heart

What is Pure Mind?

The most translated Buddhist text may well be the Dhammapada. The first two verses read as follows:

Mind runs ahead of Dharma
mind leads, mind creates.
If with impure mind
one speaks, one acts,
dukkha follows
as the wheel the hoof.

Mind runs ahead of Dharma
mind leads, mind creates.
If with pure mind
one speaks, one acts,
sukha follows
as an unfading shadow.

These verses are very famous and speak a universal, eternal wisdom. Clearly the difference between the two verses hinges on the meaning of the images in the last line and in the difference between "pure mind" and "impure mind" and between *dukkha* and *sukha*. Otherwise the verses are identical, so it is these three contrasts that are critical.

Sukha refers to bliss, dukkha to affliction, especially to the kind of afflictions and life transition points that are spiritually dangerous. When we are in a time of dukkha, we are in danger spiritually, which is to say, we are at risk of taking a corrupt path, or a path of short term gain that brings trouble in the longer run. When we are in a time of sukha, we are in safety spiritually. A hedonistic culture tends to see sukha and dukkha as pleasure and pain, or happiness and unhappiness, but this is a superficial idea. The Buddha, in a huge number of passages, warns us against spending our life chasing after pleasure and it is abundantly apparent that he was not one to shrink from hardship when this was the cost of fulfilling his mission of compassion.

An image that clearly made a big impression on his disciples because it gets referred to in the records as one that they all knew, was Buddha's simile of the two handed saw. On an occasion, when talking about anger and ill-will as corruptions of the mind, Shakyamuni said that a monk was no disciple of his if they gave way to such corruption of mind even in the circumstance where brigands had captured them and were cutting them in half with a two handed saw. It is apparent from this that Buddha's teachings are not about having an easy life or having the avoidance of painful situations as a top priority. The Buddha sent his disciples out as missionaries to carry the Dharma all over India. Later, Buddhist missionaries would travel all over Asia, even as far as Egypt. These journeys were hazardous. There is also a text in which a group of Buddhist missionaries is living with a tribe at a time when famine comes and they have to decide whether to stay and share the suffering of the local people or leave so as to reduce, by a very small degree, pressure on the dwindling food supply. They decide to stay. These and many other examples tell us that Buddhism is not the pursuit of happiness in the simple worldly sense. The happiness that Buddhism brings is that of having a pure mind. As in all great religions, Buddhism is concerned with purity of the soul ahead of considerations of personal comfort or convenience.

So it is clear that verse one refers to something, dukkha, that is toilsome and difficult and verse two to something, sukha, that is to be welcomed. We see this in the images given in the final lines. The image referred to by the phrase *as the wheel the hoof* is that of an ox cart. For the ox, the cart is a burden. It moves slowly and needs a great effort to pull along. This is an image for a burdensome life. A person who speaks and acts on the basis of impure mind has a lot of worries and finds life hard work. On the other hand, the image of the *unfading shadow* is of something effortless. The shadow, sukha, follows the person everywhere they go and makes no demand upon them other than that they stay in the sun.

It is now quite clear that the crucial point of these two verses is the contrast between pure mind and impure mind and their respective fruits. If we can understand the difference between pure and impure we shall have the meaning. At first reading, we might assume that this has something to do with moral effort. Certainly Buddhism puts emphasis on moral effort, but we need to understand the dynamic by which this occurs.

Every verse of the Dhammapada has an accompanying story. This story gives us the context in which the verse was spoken by the Buddha. The verses were later assembled into the text that we now have. When the Buddha's utterances were assembled into books the prime concern of those doing the assembling was to arrange material in a way that made it easy to remember. These two verses were put together because the parallelism and contrast between them makes them easy to remember. The occasions for the teachings, however, were different.

The story that goes with the first verse involves a monk called Cakkhupala. Cakkhupala became an arhat, but went blind. While doing walking meditation he sometimes stepped on insects. Other monks wanted to know if this brought bad karma. The Buddha said not because Cakkhupala had no intention to kill the insects. In other words, he had acted with a pure mind. The monks then wanted to know why Cakkhupala went blind and Buddha said that it was because of something done in a previous life. In that earlier life, Cakkhupala had been a doctor. A blind woman came to him and said she would be his servant if he could cure her blindness. He did so but she did not want to keep her side of the bargain. Succumbing to a selfish and vindictive impulse he gave her an ointment to put on her eyes that caused her to go blind again. This, therefore, is a story of an action based on impure mind in one life causing an effect in a subsequent life, even to a person who had become enlightened. One thing we can see from this story is that becoming an arhat, i.e. becoming enlightened, did not make Cakkhupala immune to reaping the results of past karma. Being enlightened did not eliminate dukkha. What it did do was to make Cakkhupala capable of accepting his own blindness without once again becoming vindictive.

Enlightenment means that one's mind remains pure, not that one does not suffer.

Up to this point we can retain our hypothesis that the pivotal point in these verses is to do with moral effort. If Cakkhupala had been more moral in his previous life then he would not have gone blind in this one. It looks as though this is all about karmic effect and the calculus of the merit, positive or negative, of good and bad actions. However, when we read the story connected to verse two, we find we have to modify this hypothesis in an important way.

This story concerns a boy called Mattakundali. Mattakundali becomes sick with jaundice and is close to death. His father is wealthy but stingy. Because the father is unwilling to spend money on a doctor the boy grows more and more ill and eventually dies. The Buddha, perceiving with his divine eye the plight of the boy, appears to him before his death in a vision. The boy is joyful on seeing the Buddha and thus dies with a pure heart full of faith. Consequently the boy is reborn in a heaven.

Now, in relation to our hypothesis, this story is interesting for the fact that there is really no moral effort on the part of Mattakundali other than being pleased to see the Buddha. The boy suffers as a victim of his father's meanness, but experiences sukha through the Buddha's compassion. So what is the difference between an impure mind and a pure mind? It must be clear now that an impure mind is one full of self, and a pure mind is one happily full of Buddha. With a mind full of faith in Buddha, one can die in peace. The principle in this last sentence is how East Asian people generally take the central message of Buddhism. The Dhammapada, however, is a Pali text, central to South Asian Theravada Buddhism.

Buddhism is a religion of mindfulness. The crucial point is, what is your mind full of? If the mind is full of self and selfish considerations, it is impure and such an impure mind leads to a burdensome existence full of worries and spiritual dangers. If the mind is full of one's love for and faith in a Buddha, it is a pure mind and, so long as one remains in the sunshine of Buddha's unconditional love and compassion, one will effortlessly experience a condition of spiritual safety and transcendent bliss, even if one finds oneself in dire circumstances such as dying of a readily curable disease through the meanness of others, or being captured and sawn in half with a two handed saw. This is the essential gospel of Buddhism.

This is a universal principle. This does not mean that one has to "be a Buddhist" in the sense of joining a Buddhist organisation, necessarily. When I go to interfaith meetings, as I sometimes do, I have, on a number of occasions, been asked "Is Buddha a god?" I have learnt to answer this question by saying that it does not matter whether Buddha is a god or not, but it matters a lot whether one's god is a Buddha. In general, god, or God, refers to what one has faith in and puts at the centre of one's spiritual life. If what you put there is a Buddha, which is to say, if it is loving, compassionate, sympathetic, peaceful, inclusive, kind and wise, then holding one's love for and faith in such a one will constitute pure mind. If, on the other hand, one's god, or God, were judgemental, punitive, jealous, wrathful, intolerant, or narrow-minded, then holding on to such a one will not constitute pure mind and will not bring good results. There are any number of Buddhas wearing the clothes of different cultures and speaking to people in whatever language and symbols they might be able to understand. This is not about joining a club. A pure mind transcends cultures and therefore transcends particular religions. Buddhism thus points to the essence of all true religion.

Pure mind is a function of faith and love. It is not primarily a matter of moral effort. Moral effort without faith and love tends only to make a person proud or bigoted. For moral effort to be sincere and genuine it has to have a basis in faith and love. The faith and love has to come first. If faith and love are suddenly awakened, then, naturally, there will be a gradual cultivation of self-restraint and civilised behaviour, because there is then a correct motivation. Nor is pure mind created by some technical psychological procedure. It is good to reflect on life and to appreciate the things that one encounters, it is good to have an open mind and a big heart, but all these flow naturally from having humility about oneself coupled to faith in what is best. In Buddhism, what is best is the Dharma, and the Dharma is embodied in Buddha.

When we have faith in Buddha and Dharma we are devotees. It does not have to be Shakyamuni Buddha – it could be any Buddha, but such faith is the foundation of religion. With such a foundation, our approach is religious, and when we are assembled together we become part of the eternal sangha made up of all those who have had such faith throughout time and space. To be members of this sangha we do not have to have overcome all human foibles. We are accepted as the fallible beings that we are. Even though we are foolish and vulnerable, we become part of the Buddha's dispensation, and can have a sense of limitless assurance. This assurance is not grounded in our own achievement, but in the simple faith we have in a goodness and wisdom that goes far beyond our own.

The story of Mattakundali symbolically displays the basic attitude of religion. Mattakundali is face to face with the existential human situation. He is going to die. In this extremity he meets the Buddha. This has come about because the Buddha reaches out to him. It is thus an example of grace rather than achievement. Mattakundali rejoices. Thus faith is born and spiritual salvation assured, even though the body dies.

Religion is Human

Religion is our way of relating to the unconditioned. Through this relationship life becomes satisfying and meaningful. We ourselves live in a world of conditions. We are mortal and we shall die. Nonetheless, we intuit a domain of ultimate truth. We experience love that is conditional, but we intuit unconditional love, and we have instinctive faith in it. The collective expression of this faith is religion and it centres on our faith in those who have most truly embodied it. This is not a superfluous extra; it is an essential facet of what it is to be human that has made life meaningful throughout human history. The expression of this relationship to the sacred has taken many forms and these are the many forms of religion. A religion can transform from one religious form to another in order to accommodate worldly circumstances, but it cannot transform into a non-religion without losing its ability to give life meaning in this way.

It is a frail yet vital human activity that, nonetheless, connects us with things that are eternal, enduring and will always be true in all worlds. In our reception of Buddhism in the West we have too often missed the fact that this is what it is all about. Only a small minority of people in the West truly realise that Buddhism is concerned with nirvana and that nirvana is not just a psychological condition, but unconditioned, unborn, deathless, reality. In trying so hard to avoid the fundamental nature of this religion we deceive ourselves and miss the main thing that it has to offer.

A religion is concerned with ultimacy, but it is still a human activity. Thus what Buddha found had always been true and will always be true, but it takes a Buddha to find and transmit it. Thus we consider ourselves highly fortunate to live in a world where the Dharma has been transmitted. It is said that the transmission hangs by a thread. Although many people might consider themselves to be Buddhist, in practice the number who have complete faith is limited. A religion has a core of a few people who deeply comprehend and transmit the truth, and ever increasing circles of people who understand less and less deeply until one reaches those who make use of some bit of the Dharma, but have no understanding of its basis. Probably it will always be thus.

When an occidental person reads this, typically, they are inclined to think about how they can become members of this select core group and to look for a method to achieve this. They do not want to have faith in someone else, they want to have faith in themselves. We all want to be god. Religion, however, starts with realising that one is not god.

It is this element of arrogance that blinds us to the spirit of Buddhism. Without a deep appreciation of our own frailty, it is difficult to grasp the original spirit. It is certainly good to control the mind and act in good ways, but these accomplishments derive more from personal modesty and faith than from will-power and achievement.

When we have this kind of foundation in modesty, religion is a blessing. If people can appreciate that whatever we all-too-human beings create will itself be frail, then religions can live at peace with one another and we can all learn from each other without regarding it as a failing to do so. If Buddhists could see that Jesus may also be a Buddha and if Christians could see that Buddha may also be a saviour, then peace and harmony could reign and we could all enjoy our different offerings.

Religion is faith on one's own and it is faith together. These are two basic aspects of religion. Religious faith sustains us when all else fails and religious faith unites us when we stand together. Thus religion is personal courage and it is also loving community. People who have such faith and such community tend to be good and happy people. Buddhism, however, is not simply a way of inducing people to be good or even of making them happy. These things are natural fruits of faith, but faith may also make difficult demands.

The same is true with belief. Faith leads one to have different beliefs about the world because it leads one to take a long term view. Nonetheless, people with equally strong faith do not all, necessarily, believe exactly the same things. We need to distinguish between the fruit and the root. Too often people have taken the fruits of religion to be the whole of it. This has led to two different kinds of error. On the one hand it can lead to the kind of asset stripping approach that we currently see a lot of, where people think that they can take aspects of the religion and strip them of their religious nature and context. By this type of approach one can certainly get something, but what one gets is a poor replica, a bit like having a plastic Christmas tree rather than a real pine. The second type of error is that of thinking that because religion leads people to be morally good, all that is needed is to teach them good from bad and enforce good behaviour. This second kind of error misses the point of religion just as much as the first one does. This is true whether the "good behaviour" is "Thou shalt not steal," "Thou shalt meditate every day," or even "Thou shalt live in the here and now." Religion cannot be reduced to a technique or protocol. At the core of religion is faith and this is just as true of Buddhism as it is of any other religion.

Another way of saying the same thing is to say that Buddhism is about non-self. Faith is the opposite of reliance upon one's own ego and self-power. Attempting to rely upon oneself one falls into guilt and anxiety because one is never good enough, or, alternatively, one becomes blind to one's own shortcomings and seeks to exploit others. Recently, in popular psychology, there has been a good deal of advocacy of the idea of loving oneself. It was believed that since people suffer from feeling unloved, the answer is for them to love themselves. This is really something of a counsel of despair. The religious person does not need to love him or herself because they have confidence in being deeply loved already.

Linked to this is the idea of self-esteem. Heightened self-esteem is the goal of many contemporary popular psychology programmes. This is a modern phenomenon. If you look at books more than fifty years old you find no mention of it. Indeed, in the past, it would have been called narcissism and regarded as a problem. Working as a psychotherapist in recent times I have had quite a large number of clients who came to me saying that they have such-and-such a personal problem, and then adding that they already understand that the problem is that they do not love themselves enough, or that they lack self-esteem. We seem to have reached the crazy position where many people feel additional guilt because they are failing in the task of loving themselves. There is no need for this.

The strength of religion is that it does not ask us to rely entirely upon ourselves. We could distinguish several levels of religion. Since religion is always a human creation and a human activity, even if it is reaching out toward something ultimate and perfect, religion itself can never be perfect. It can only be human. Nonetheless, the best religion will be one where the reliance upon ultimate truth is most complete. Since such truth is universal and eternal, such faith will be all-pervasive and could take a limitless number of forms. This is the faith of great mystics.

The next level of faith, slightly less pure, but still inspiring, is one in which devotees keep the object of refuge always in mind, or, at least, in mind as much as possible. This is the path of investigation of the truth based on mindfulness, in the sense that the term mindfulness has been used in this book, namely that of keeping holy things in mind: in the case of a Buddhist, keeping Buddha, Dharma and Sangha in mind. Those who have this kind of faith are those who have met Buddha one way or another in the course of their life. This encounter has touched them to such a depth that their lives can never be the same again. They are like Mattakundali.

The next level could be one in which the devotees have a practice, which might be prayer, or meditation, or some other ceremonial form. They have faith that doing the practice will result in good things. They may not have met the Buddha directly, but they have been influenced by other people who have stronger faith and they want some of the benefits. Alternatively this level could be one in which, following their own intuition, a person lives a morally upright life, adhering to a code of conduct, feeling secure that this is the best way to live. Again, such a faith is derivative, but it can still bring good karma.

We are corrupt human beings. Therefore, our religion is always corrupt in some degree and it is even corrupt to count degrees of corruption. All religion is human and therefore imperfect and it is only when we realise this imperfection that we can learn from and celebrate one another. Religion is grounded in humility about human nature and the human condition. We have lost faith in religion because religion fell into the corruption of arrogance, which was the very disease it was intended to attend to. We have lost the doctor because the doctor fell prey to the disease he was supposed to cure.

Religion that considers itself to be perfect becomes intolerant of its neighbours. Their very existence threatens to demonstrate its own blindness. This has been a path to hell. However, that we have ruined religion by descending into arrogant intolerance does not imply that what we have corrupted was not pure in the first place, only that we are what we are and we are in need of doing something better. Rather than throwing out the idea of religion and trying to live by our wits, it will be much healthier for the human race to rehabilitate the idea of religion as a fundamental part of what it is to be human, yet make the transition to a world in which we are all neighbours.

Mattakundali died happy and full of faith. This was not the result of years of disciplined practice. It was the result of meeting the Buddha. Buddhist texts are full of such encounters. If we can appreciate the moral of this story we will save ourselves a lot of unnecessary trouble.

13: The Need for Religious Buddhism

The Awakening of Faith

One of the most important books in the history of Buddhism is called *The Awakening of Faith in the Great Vehicle*, written by a sage called Ashvaghosha.

Buddhism has to be faith rather than mere technique because technique is always grasping after something, whereas faith is stopping, looking and receiving. Buddhism is stopping (*samatha*), looking (*vipassana*) and receiving (*sarana*). If we cannot stop, we will not receive.

There is no technique by which spiritual awakening can be hunted down or trapped in a net. You can go out with your net and you might catch a fish, but spiritual awakening is not the fish, it is the water, and the water will always slip through your net. Even though it is already all around you, you will not notice the water if your mind is focussed on catching a fish. However, if you catch the fish and take it out of the water it will soon be dead and in a day or two it will begin to smell bad.

Religion is like seeing the water. Grace is already all around us, behind us and ahead of us. It is not just in the here and now, it is in the always everywhere. However, simply knowing as knowledge that the Dharmakaya is always everywhere does not, in itself, ensure that one will have faith in it and entrust one's life to it. A mere idea does not suffice. Knowing about religion hardly constitutes one inch of real faith. This is why an academic study of religion will not save one. You can read a thousand books and still not have given rise to real religion. Yet, in a moment of faith one stops fishing and suddenly the sea is all around, extending endlessly in every direction.

If we study Buddhism from the outside we see Buddhists doing all manner of things. We see some people doing acts of charity, some people meditating in caves, some people doing elaborate rituals, people campaigning on political issues, people building temples and carving statues, people happily living the lives of peasants in the foothills of the Himalayas, others making sites on the internet or networking using electronic media, we see groups chanting or singing and scholars in libraries researching ancient texts, people adhering to strict disciplines and others engaged in artistic creativity. If we have only an external view we are liable to say: what is Buddhism? Is Buddhism just a collection of widely diverse activities? We cannot say that it is one activity, for it manifests as many activities. We cannot say that it is one lifestyle, because some Buddhists are celibate and some have children, some live as hermits and some in communities, some are rich and some are poor. We cannot even say it is a single doctrine or philosophy, for Buddhism has many doctrines and has given rise to many philosophies. It continues to do so. To the external view Buddhism is an assemblage of many things and one might see it as ever changing and adapting to new circumstances.

To the inside view, however, all these activities clearly emerge from a common spirit and that spirit is religious. The core of spiritual awakening does not change.

It may wear different clothes in different climes, but it remains the same. It is like ocean water which may flow into seas and bays, straits and channels of many shapes and sizes but still always has the same salt taste. This is the nature of religion. We have tried to say that Buddhism is not a religion in part to satisfy a modern prejudice and in part as a marketing strategy. Religion having fallen into disrepute in many areas of modern life, it made sense to present Buddhism as a non-religion to avoid giving rise to undue resistance. After all, it was not Buddhist religion that people had turned away from, so why should Buddhism have to carry the burden of facing the resulting opposition?

European colonialism in Asia threatened to destroy Buddhism and replace it with Christianity. However, at that time, the colonial powers were themselves struggling with the debate in Europe that had polarised science and religion and science was winning the debate. Those who sought to defend Buddhism against the encroachment of Christianity, therefore, prudently allied Buddhism with science. Buddhist texts were purged of anything that sounded incompatible with science and the Dharma was presented as scientific spirituality. This contributed to an emerging distinction between religion and spirituality that has nowadays reached the point where many people will identify themselves as "spiritual but not religious," which is close to being a contradiction of terms, but meets the felt need to retain spiritual sensitivity while distancing oneself from the arrogance, oppression and bigotry that had come to be associated with some of the traditional religions and is still associated with some fundamentalists of various creeds.

The alliance with science has served Buddhism well up to a point. It has made western people much more willing to consider engaging in Buddhist activities, especially meditation and, latterly, with a form of mindfulness. This has smoothed the way to a general acceptance that Buddhism is a peaceful creed with something important to offer to the modern world. So far so good. However, there has also been a downside. This has been the cost to Buddhism of dropping or hiding much of what it has traditionally consisted and importing many attitudes and values that do not belong to it, but are expressions of the reductionism of modernity on the one hand and of a Western preoccupation with problems bequeathed by Christianity on the other.

Tibetan Buddhism would appear to have compromised least, even though it too has had to make substantial concessions. This has been achieved by the fact that Tibetan Buddhism has appealed more to the romantic than the scientific side of Western culture. Many traditions have thus survived as forms of exoticism where in other forms of Buddhism, such as Theravada, for instance, the reform has been more ruthless. This is because the earliest stages of this rationalising reform commenced in the Theravada countries that were colonised by European powers. At that time confidence in modernity was at its peak. Since then, while it remains the core element in much Western culture, it has, nonetheless, declined. This is in part because, as mentioned earlier, most of the goals of modernism have not come to pass and in part because the humanistic, progressive, technology-based project can readily be seen not just to have produced domestic convenience and modern medicine, but also the destruction of the environment, nuclear weapons, and such disasters as Chernobyl and Fukushima. Tibetan Buddhism did not experience any substantial exposure to such modernism until the mid-twentieth century. Its survival strategy has been correspondingly different.

So, Buddhism has given up a good deal in its struggle to survive and renew itself in an age dominated by a gradually declining "modernistic" rationalism. When modernity was at its peak, survival was only possible through an alliance with it and, strategically, Buddhism did well to make an alliance with science in the face of Christian missionary efforts. However, with modernism now in decline, there is a danger that a modernist Buddhism will decline with it. A Buddhism that has been reduced to a string of technical novelties cannot be expected to have great staying power. Techniques adopted by professionals for particular ends can be picked up and put down again with relative ease and the whole process is strongly affected by changes of fashion. What is in favour this month may be out again next. The professional user has some identification with the technique he or she is employing, but it does not run as deep as the identification that a religious devotee has with their faith. Buddhism is becoming more widespread, but is in danger of losing its depth. Buddhism itself makes life meaningful; it is not a set of methods to make other meanings viable.

Buddhism Can Change Us

In the past, in Asia, the transmission of the Dharma relied heavily on the existence of large numbers of, usually celibate, monks. Nowadays, even though Buddhism has undergone a revival in many Asian countries at the same time as it has been becoming popular in the West, the number of such monks is still in decline. The sangha is one of the three core refuges of Buddhism. If the sangha declines, Buddhism is in danger.

Whether such a celibate sangha can regenerate itself or not is an open question. Not all religions have based themselves on such a celibate clergy. What is essential, however, is a strong core of people who do have a level and depth of commitment that one can only adequately describe as religious. Professional use of Buddhist methods, academic study of Buddhist texts and history, popular adoption of Buddhist icons and symbols, and even large scale attendance at retreats led by Buddhist figures who have attained celebrity status, can all contribute to creating conditions in which Buddhism can grow and flourish, but they are epiphenomena. At the core there has to be religious dedication or Buddhism will pass into history.

We have to see Buddhism as restoring religion to its proper course rather than allowing our degenerated concept of religion to tarnish Buddhism. True religion is grounded in faith, humility and gratitude. The association with science and scientism has too often led modern Buddhist apologists to make arrogant claims for the effectiveness of their technical expertise when what the world needed was a display of genuine humanity and humility. What has often been of greater long term value has been the demeanour of Asian Buddhists. It is not so much what they have said to us as simply the way that they are that has occasioned a stir and challenged our assumptions. The most effective apologist for Buddhism in this period has, without doubt, been the Dalai Lama, whose openness, tolerance, urbanity and message of "My religion is kindness" has touched many hearts.

I feel that what is happening at the moment is that the West is trying to assimilate this disturbance. Assimilation means taking it in with minimum modification of the pre-existing paradigm. This is not what is needed. Buddhism offers a challenge to the paradigm at the root. If we sidestep this challenge we miss a huge opportunity.

History is at a new juncture on at least three counts. Full scale war between the major countries is now impractical because the level of destruction would be so universal that there would be no victor. This has never been the case before. Communication technology has now reached a level where the whole planet is becoming a single community to an unprecedented degree. Thirdly, we are becoming aware that collectively we are in danger of destroying the biosphere. These three factors mean that there has to be a deep level change in the way that we think, feel and relate to one another.

Some people think that this deep change should be one in which religion disappears. This would be the logical extension of the idea of modernity that thinks that the new situation is best tackled scientifically and rationally by a secularist approach. However, it is the ideas of modernity that have created many of the problems we currently face.

My suggestion in this book is that rather than abandoning religion, what we need is actually a deeper religious consciousness and that this can be found in the perennial wisdom of Buddha. In this new historical situation institutions are changing. Buddhist institutions will also change, but let us not lose the essence of the

Dharma in the process. Let us be part of a higher evolution of faith that expands our hearts and minds rather than narrowing them. Buddhism is a religion that welcomes science and is not opposed to rational social administration, but which is not limited to them. It offers liberation through devotion to higher things. It is not enough for us to live for the moment and neglect the long term effect. We need to place what is truly wise, kind and sacred at the core of our lives and have the courage to live the kind of simple yet noble existence that does not gobble up all the world's resources, exterminate other species, arrange everything for our own convenience, and revolve around fame and gain. Buddhism offers a gentler way and to be grasped by it we need to see that its essence is religious in nature.

Organised Spirituality

Religion is organised spirituality. Buddhism is certainly a religion in this sense. The organisation may be of many kinds. A fortunate by-product of modern developments is that a large proportion of Western Buddhists are internet literate and Buddhism has a presence in the internet out of proportion to the size of its following. It may well be that Buddhism will turn the tables on modernity in the end. By this I mean that whereas at present we see persons of a secular rational outlook cherry picking methods from Buddhism to use in the service of their own technical agendas, it may well be that Buddhism will succeed by deploying the technological fruits of modern science to evolve a new style of religious organisation. The image of the monk with a Macbook is an instantly recognisable icon of this new approach.

Modern communications have allowed socially diverse elements to come together in ways that would have been impossible until recently. This could lead to a general dilution of all principle or commitment, but it could also be the making of fertile spaces where great creativity becomes possible. Which way this goes will be a function of the commitments of the people involved.

Buddhist organisation in the West has unfortunately tended to follow the model of Western sectarianism which originally came about in the fragmentation of Protestantism in the centuries following the European Reformation. In a city like Los Angeles one can find more than a hundred brands of Buddhism each having, or striving to obtain, their own temple where they can practice their own rituals, celebrated by their own lineage of monks or priests, wearing their own distinctive costumes, and holding on to their own congregation in an exclusivist manner. Often there is little or no co-operation between such groups and, not infrequently, even ignorance of each other's existence. Each proposes that what it does and teaches is Buddhism, as if it were the only form in existence. It is rather strange that so many of these groups, organised on such traditional (to the West) ecclesial lines, continue to assert that they are not a religion.

After experiencing Buddhism in the West, in my travels in Asia I was pleasantly surprised to find little emphasis on the importance of lineage, a subject seldom mentioned, and considerably less, though by no means a complete absence of, sectarianism. There is a real danger that Buddhism is being weakened by the extent to which it has been infected by such division. It was a powerful experience for me when I visited Vietnam and managed to obtain an interview with the Venerable Master Minh Chao, and heard him say "All Buddhism is good." He was, at that time, the principal of a training school for monks and nuns in which the teaching staff were representative of all the eleven schools of Buddhism found in Vietnam.

Historically, Buddhism has always been an organised spirituality, and therefore a religion, but the form of organisation has changed with the times and the climes. Times when Buddhism has flourished have often been those when great Buddhist universities were not only seats of learning and venues for the transmission of received doctrine, but were also centres for debate as well as experimentation and development in the modes of transmission of the Dharma. One thinks of Vasubandhu, one of the pivotal figures in the history of the religion, changing from one persuasion within Buddhism to another as a result of exposure to such a maelstrom of thought, practice and principles.

The internet and modern travel now allow the possibility of creating new ferments of this kind. It is important that we cherish this kind of opportunity and not allow it to frighten us into narrow mindedness or retreat into overly fixed positions. Buddhism must restore the capacity of religion to be the place where the most important issues in human life are explored in a lively, compassionate and mutually respectful way. This is not just a matter of how Buddhists relate to other faiths. It is about how we conduct ourselves within the Buddhist community itself.

The establishment of a hundred varieties of Buddhism in Los Angeles or London or wherever is a product of a desire to retain the purity of traditions emanating from Asia. When each group consists of quite a small number of people, this task can consume all the available energy. A degree of rigidity is thus understandable. To have got to this point in the transmission of the Dharma to the West is an achievement worth celebrating. However, this is like the warp in a loom. We now need some weft to pull it all together and turn these individual strands into a resilient cloth.

I am optimistic that this will happen and I expect that it will occur in ways that are new and relevant to our contemporary way of life. This will take us beyond secular rationalism and will enable us to rebuild, or build anew, genuinely tender spiritual community, not merely retain Buddhism as a commodity. Buddhism will thus be a new kind of religion, giving meaning to our lives through a spirit that is ages old, but doing so in ways that accord with contemporary technology and usage. Buddhism must use the technology, not be used by it, must pull it together rather than be fragmented by it. This will not happen by Buddhism adopting the values of self-interest, instrumentalism, utilitarianism, capitalism or communism. It will happen by the Buddhist values of humility, respect, faith, compassion, loving kindness, sympathy, and refuge finding new confidence in these new circumstances. They are what the world needs. To gain attention in the contemporary world it may be necessary for Buddhism to throw up some charismatic leaders, but if they then become subsumed into the individualistic competition of celebrities that prevails in contemporary media it will have been in vain.

We are at an unprecedented nexus in history. In the past, in political matters, war was always available as a final resort. War was terrible, but it did have some degree of cleansing effect, sweeping away old social structures that had become moribund and allowing a new start. Modern warfare is now so destructive that one can no longer imagine Europe going to war with America or Russia, say, and, increasingly, it is going to become the case that full scale war is no longer a practical option. How, therefore, are we going to cleanse our social life of accumulations of moribund structures and creeping corruption? We need a purer spirit running through the core of our society. We need the Buddhist ideal of Dharmaraja – of enlightened government. I am not saying that Buddhism should become the established religion of our countries, though in some cases that could happen eventually. I mean rather that for society to function in a compassionate rather than in a purely mechanical manner, there needs to be an injection of such a spirit as lies at the core of Buddhism and for that to happen there need to be people who have a religious degree of commitment to those values and insights. This is what Shakyamuni tried to do.

Buddhism was not originally conceived as a universal religion, out to convert everybody, so much as a project to create a cadre of people deeply dedicated to the Dharma, who would be a leaven in society. *There will be a few with little dust in their eyes, who are wasting through not hearing the Dharma.* These were the words of the god, Brahma Sahampati, that sent Shakyamuni forth into the world to spread the Dharma in the first place. It is the same today.

The Buddhist practitioner, wandering from place to place, teaching kings and commoners alike, was an influence at all levels of society. He or she inspired a higher morale, one that permeated the body social. This inspiration flowed more from the example of pure living that was manifested than from the content of the teaching given. Here were people who were not interested in personal gain, who wanted only the wellbeing of others, who mediated in disputes, who spoke words worthy to be laid up in the heart, who were humble and neither offensive nor defensive. They were able to be so because they were grounded in the Dharma, the ultimate radiance from which arises unconditional love.

Our world needs such emissaries of the Dharma. Nowadays they may wear different clothes and travel by different means, but the message will remain, the spirit of such lives remains the same; the Dharma does not change and at this turning point in history we need it more than ever before. For the world to have it, some of us must have the courage to believe in it to such a degree that it becomes the organising hub of our life. It has to be our religion and we should have no shame in presenting it as such.

About David Brazier

David Brazier, whose Buddhist name 'Dharmavidya' means "clear perception of what is fundamental", is a travelling Buddhist teacher, authority on Buddhist psychology, President of the Instituto Terapia Zen Internacional, Head of the Order of Amida Buddha, Spiritual Guide of the Eleusis Centre, Patron of the Tathagata Trust, scholar, doctor of philosophy (PhD), Buddhist priest, author of nine previous books, psychotherapist, social worker, published poet ("Her Mother's Eyes & Other Poems"), inventor of pandramatics, the other centred approach and Zen Therapy, founder of spiritual communities, international traveller, inspirational lecturer and philanthropist. He was fortunate to encounter leading Buddhist teachers at the beginning of his adult life and their teachings spoke to his condition. He travels widely and has been the creator of aid, education and social work projects in Europe, India and elsewhere and of training programmes in Buddhist psychology, Zen Therapy and Buddhist ministry. His books include works on psychotherapy and on Buddhism and commentary on the relationship between spirituality, art, myth and culture. He has three adult children, five grandchildren, likes gardening, walking and photography and lives in France.

www.ingramcontent.com/pod-product-compliance
Ingram Content Group UK Ltd.
Pitfield, Milton Keynes, MK11 3LW, UK
UKHW020226250726
13967UKWH00001B/217